Wall and Floor Tiling

CONSTRUCTION SERIES

Wall and Floor Tiling

CONSTRUCTION SERIES

Australia • Brazil • Japan • Korea • Mexico • Singapore • Spain • United Kingdom • United States

Wall and Floor Tiling
Skills2Learn

Publishing Director: Linden Harris
Commissioning Editor: Lucy Mills
Development Editor: Helen Green
Editorial Assistant: Claire Napoli
Project Editor: Lucy Arthy
Production Controller: Eyvett Davis
Marketing Manager: Jason Bennett
Typesetter: MPS Limited, a Macmillan Company
Cover design: HCT Creative
Text design: Design Deluxe

© 2012 Cengage Learning EMEA

ALL RIGHTS RESERVED. No part of this work covered by the copyright herein may be reproduced, transmitted, stored or used in any form or by any means graphic, electronic, or mechanical, including but not limited to photocopying, recording, scanning, digitizing, taping, Web distribution, information networks, or information storage and retrieval systems, except as permitted under Section 107 or 108 of the 1976 United States Copyright Act, or applicable copyright law of another jurisdiction, without the prior written permission of the publisher.

While the publisher has taken all reasonable care in the preparation of this book, the publisher makes no representation, express or implied, with regard to the accuracy of the information contained in this book and cannot accept any legal responsibility or liability for any errors or omissions from the book or the consequences thereof.

Products and services that are referred to in this book may be either trademarks and/or registered trademarks of their respective owners. The publishers and author/s make no claim to these trademarks.

The publisher does not endorse, and accepts no responsibility or liability for, incorrect or defamatory content contained in hyperlinked material.

For product information and technology assistance,
contact **emea.info@cengage.com**.
For permission to use material from this text or product,
and for permission queries,
email **emea.permissions@cengage.com**.

DISCLAIMER

This publication has been developed by Cengage Learning. It is intended as a method of studying and to assist in training in relation to its subject matter and should be used only as part of a comprehensive training programme with tutor guidance. Cengage Learning has taken all reasonable care in the preparation of this publication but Cengage learning and Skills2Learn and its partners accept no liability howsoever in respect of any breach of the rights of any third party howsoever occasioned or damage caused to any third party as a result of this publication. The information contained in the publication is not a substitute for manufacturer's guidelines or current legislation. Cengage Learning and Skills2Learn and its partners do not endorse or recommend any of the proprietary products that may be named in the publication.

British Library Cataloguing-in-Publication Data

A catalogue record for this book is available from the British Library.

ISBN: 978-1-4080-4189-5

Cengage Learning EMEA

Cheriton House, North Way, Andover, Hampshire, SP10 5BE
United Kingdom

Cengage Learning products are represented in Canada by Nelson Education Ltd.

For your lifelong learning solutions, visit **www.cengage.co.uk**

Purchase your next print book, e-book or e-chapter at **www.cengagebrain.com**

Printed in Malta by Melita Press
1 2 3 4 5 6 7 8 9 10 – 14 13 12

Contents

Foreword vi
About the Construction Consortia vii
About e-learning viii
About the NOS xiii
About the book xiv

1 Getting started 1

Introduction 2
Backgrounds 6
Communication 16
Check your knowledge 17

2 Materials 19

Tiles 20
Adhesives and grout 24
Spacers and trims 27
Tools 30
Ordering materials 43
Storage of materials 47
Disposal of materials 48
Check your knowledge 50

3 Setting out 53

Setting out floor tiles 54
Setting out wall tiles 59
Check your knowledge 69

4 Applying tiles 71

Laying and applying tiles 72
Cutting tiles 82
Grouting 97
Trade tips 101
Check your knowledge 102

5 End test 103

End test objectives 103
The test 104

Answers to check your knowledge and end test 108
Glossary 113
Index 116

Foreword

The construction industry is a significant part of the UK economy and a major employer of people. It has a huge impact on the environment and plays a role on our everyday life in some shape or form. With environmental issues such as climate change and sustainable sourcing of materials now playing an important part in the design and construction of buildings and other structures, there is a need to educate and re-educate those new to the industry and those currently involved.

This construction series of e-learning programmes and text workbooks have been developed to provide a structured blended learning approach that will enhance the learning experience and stimulate a deeper understanding of the construction trades and give an awareness of sustainability issues. The content within these learning materials has been aligned to units of the Wall and Floor Tiling, National Occupational Standards and can be used as a support tool whilst studying for any relevant vocational qualifications.

The uniqueness of this construction series is that it aims to bridge the gap between classroom-based and practical-based learning. The workbooks provide classroom-based activities that can involve learners in discussions and research tasks as well as providing them with understanding and knowledge of the subject. The e-learning programmes take the subject further, with high quality images, animations and audio further enhancing the content and showing information in a different light. In addition, the e-practical side of the e-learning places the learner in a virtual environment where they can move around freely, interact with objects and use the knowledge and skills they have gained from the workbook and e-learning to complete a set of tasks whilst in the comfort of a safe working environment.

The workbooks and e-learning programmes are designed to help learners continuously improve their skills and provide confidence and a sound knowledge base before getting their hands dirty in the real world.

About the Construction Consortia

This series of construction workbooks and e-learning programmes have been developed by the E-Construction Consortium. The consortium is a group of colleges and organizations that are passionate about the construction industry and are determined to enhance the learning experiences of people within the different trades or those that are new to it.

The consortium members have many years experience in the construction and educational sectors and have created this blended learning approach of interactive e-learning programmes and text workbooks to achieve the aim of:

- Providing accessible training in different areas of construction.
- Bridging the gap between classroom-based and practical-based learning.
- Providing a concentrated set of improvement learning modules.
- Enabling learners to gain new skills and qualifications more effectively.
- Improving functional skills and awareness of sustainability issues within the industry.
- Promoting health and safety in the industry.
- Encouraging training and continuous professional development.

For more information about this construction series please visit: www.e-construction.co.uk or www.skills2learn.com.

About e-learning

INTRODUCTION

This construction series of workbooks and e-learning programmes use a blended learning approach to train learners in construction skills. Blended learning allows training to be delivered through different mediums such as books, e-learning (computer-based training), practical workshops, and traditional classroom techniques. These training methods are designed to complement each other and work in tandem to achieve overall learning objectives and outcomes.

E-LEARNING

The Wall and Floor Tiling e-learning programme that is also available to sit alongside this workbook offers a different method of learning. With technology playing an increasingly important part of everyday life, e-learning uses visually rich 2D and 3D graphics/animation, audio, video, text and interactive quizzes, to allow you to engage with the content and learn at your own pace and in your own time.

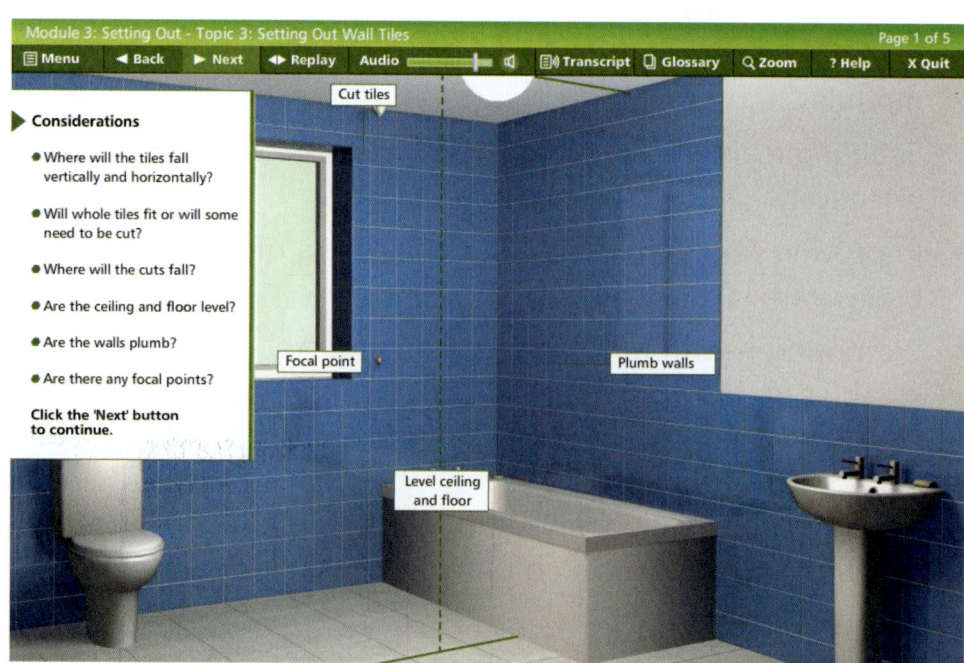

E-PRACTICAL

Part of the e-learning programme is an e-practical interactive scenario. This facility allows you to be immersed in a virtual reality situation where the choices you make affect the outcome. Using 3D technology, you can move freely around the environment, interact with objects, carry out tests, and make decisions and mistakes until you have mastered the subject. By practising in a virtual environment you will not only be able to see what you've learnt but also analyze your approach and thought process to the problem.

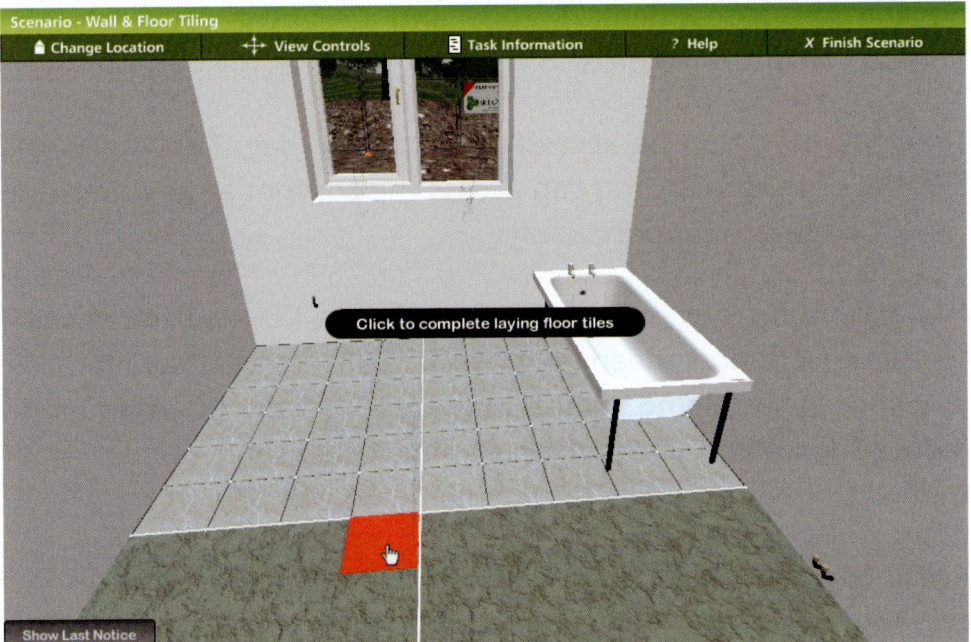

BENEFITS OF E-LEARNING

Diversity – E-Learning can be used for almost anything. With the correct approach any subject can be brought to life to provide an interactive training experience.

Technology – Advancements in computer technology now allow a wide range of spectacular and engaging e-learning to be delivered to a wider population.

ABOUT E-LEARNING

Captivate and Motivate – Hold the learners attention for longer with the use of high quality graphics, animation, sound and interactivity.

Safe Environment – E-Practical scenarios can create environments which simulate potentially harmful real-life situations or replicate a piece of dangerous equipment, therefore allowing the learner to train and gain experience and knowledge in a completely safe environment.

Instant Feedback – Learners can undertake training assessments that feed back results instantly. This can provide information on where they need to re-study or congratulate them on passing the assessment. Results and Certificates can also be printed for future records.

On-Demand – Can be accessed 24 hours a day, 7 days a week, 365 days of the year. You can access the content at any time and view it at your own pace.

Portable Solutions – Can be delivered via a CD, website or LMS. Learners no longer need to travel to all lectures, conferences, meetings or training days. This saves many man-hours in reduced travelling, cost of hotels and expenses amongst other things.

Reduction of Costs – Can be used to teach best practice processes on jobs which use large quantities or expensive materials. Learners can practise their techniques and boost their confidence to a high enough standard before being allowed near real materials.

WALL AND FLOOR TILING E-LEARNING

The aim of the wall and floor tiling e-learning programme is to enhance a learner's knowledge and understanding of the tiling trade. The course content is aligned to units from the Wall and

Floor Tiling; National Occupational Standards (NOS) so can be used for study towards certification.

The programme gives the learners an understanding of the technicalities of tiling as well as looking at sustainability, health and safety and functional skills in an interactive and visually engaging manner. It also provides a 'real-life' scenario where the learner can apply the knowledge gained from the tutorials in a safe yet practical way.

By using and completing this programme, it is expected that learners will:

- Be able to explain why tiling is an important part of the construction process.
- Understand the preliminary checks that need to be carried out before tiling can start.
- Be able to explain the choice of materials for a project, calculate the correct quantities, source these from an appropriate supplier and identify the correct disposal method for waste materials.
- Understand the processes involved in measuring and setting out.
- Be able to explain the processes involved in floor and wall tiling.

The e-learning programme is divided into the following learning modules:

- Getting Started
- Materials
- Setting Out
- Applying Tiles
- End Test
- Interactive E-Practical Scenario

THE CONSTRUCTION SERIES

As part of the construction series the following e-learning programmes and workbooks are available. For more information please contact the sales team on **emea.fesales@cengage.com** or visit the website **www.e-construction.co.uk**.

- Plastering
- Bricklaying
- Carpentry & Joinery
- Painting & Decorating
- Wall & Floor Tiling

About the NOS

The National Occupational Standards (NOS) provide a framework of information that outline the skills, knowledge and understanding required to carry out work-based activities within a given vocation. Each standard is divided into units that cover specific activities of that occupation. Employers, employees, teachers and learners can use these standards as an information, support and reference resource that will enable them to understand the skills and criteria required for good practice in the workplace.

The standards are used as a basis to develop many vocational qualifications in the United Kingdom for a wide range of occupations. This workbook and associated e-learning programme are aligned to the Wall and Floor Tiling, National Occupational Standards, and the information within relates to the following units:

- Conform to General Workplace Safety
- Conform to Efficient Work Practices
- Move and Handle Resources
- Prepare Backgrounds for Tiling
- Tile Wall and Floor Surfaces
- Produce Tiled, Mosaic and Stone Surface Finishes
- Provide Drainage for Tiled Surfaces
- Lay Undertile Heating Systems and Tile Surfaces
- Confirm Work Activities and Resources for the Work
- Develop and Maintain Good Working Relationships

About the book

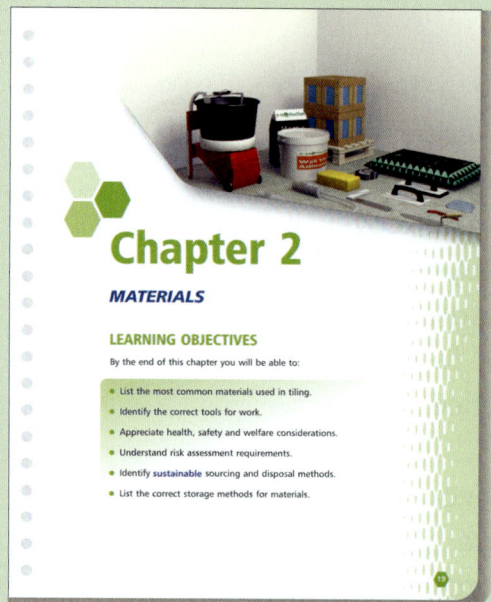

Learning Objectives at the start of each chapter explain the skills and knowledge you need to be proficient in and understand by the end of the chapter.

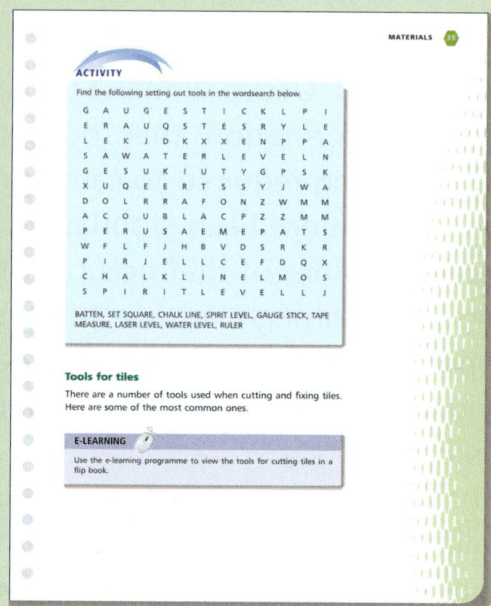

Activities are practical tasks that engage you in the subject and further your understanding.

E-Learning Icons link the workbook content to the e-learning programme.

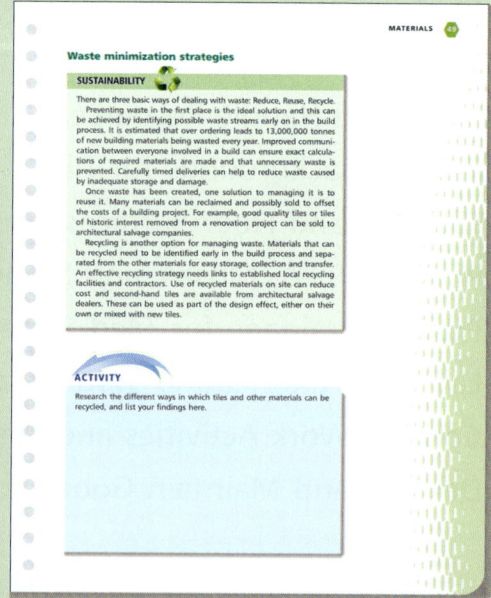

Sustainability Boxes provide information and helpful advice on how to work in a sustainable and environmentally friendly way.

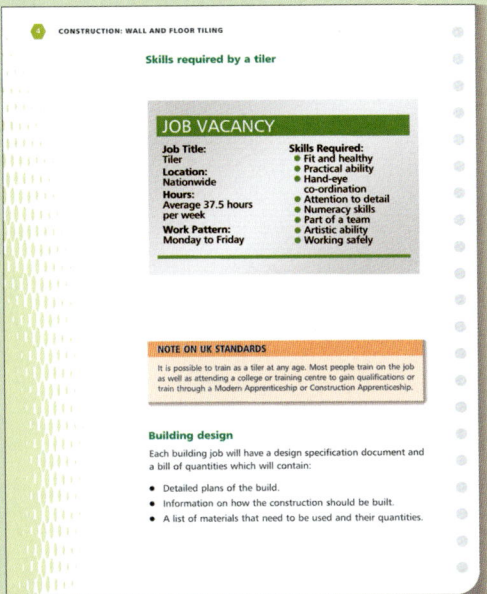

Note on UK Standards draws your attention to relevant building regulations.

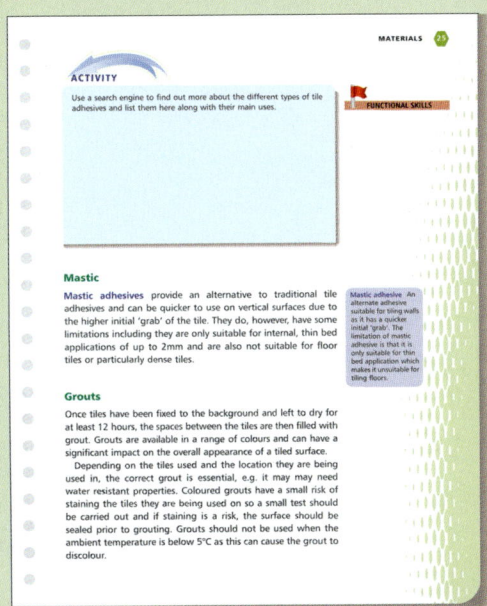

Functional Skills Icons highlight activities that develop and test your Maths, English and ICT key skills.

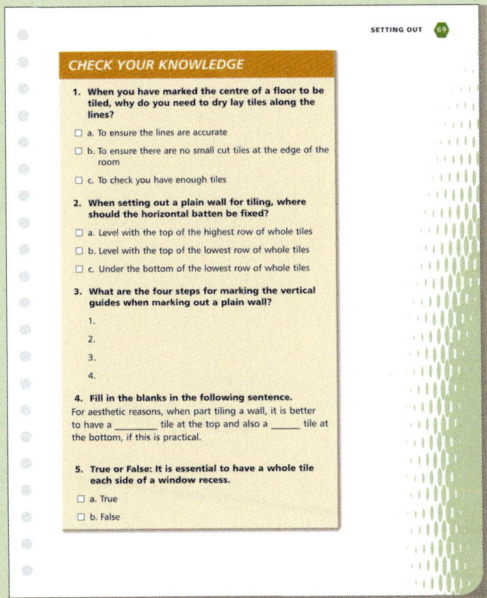

Check Your Knowledge at the end of each chapter to test your knowledge and understanding.

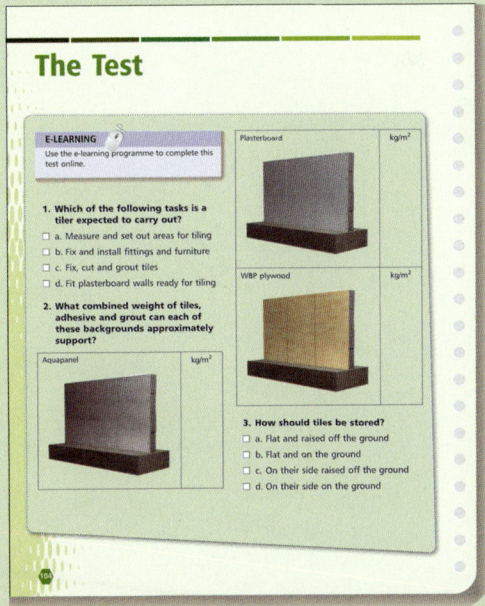

End Test in Chapter 6 checks your knowledge on all the information within the workbook.

Chapter 1

GETTING STARTED

LEARNING OBJECTIVES

By the end of this chapter you will be able to:

- Explain why we tile and why it is such an important part of the construction process.

- Understand what **backgrounds** are suitable for tiling, their tolerances and the treatment of these backgrounds prior to tiling.

- Understand where tiling fits into the overall construction process and the importance of communication with other trades.

CONSTRUCTION: WALL AND FLOOR TILING

> **Backgrounds** General term used for the surface to which materials are adhered.

NOS REFERENCE

Prepare backgrounds for tiling

Lay undertile heating systems and tile surfaces

Confirm work activities and resources for the work

Conform to efficient work practices

Develop and maintain good working relationships

> **Grout** A cement-based filler, available in a range of colours and formulated with varying sized fine aggregates to fill the joints between tiles. Some grouts can be waterproof.

INTRODUCTION

The role of the tiler

Tiling is carried out in the second fix stage of construction which means it happens towards the end of a project.

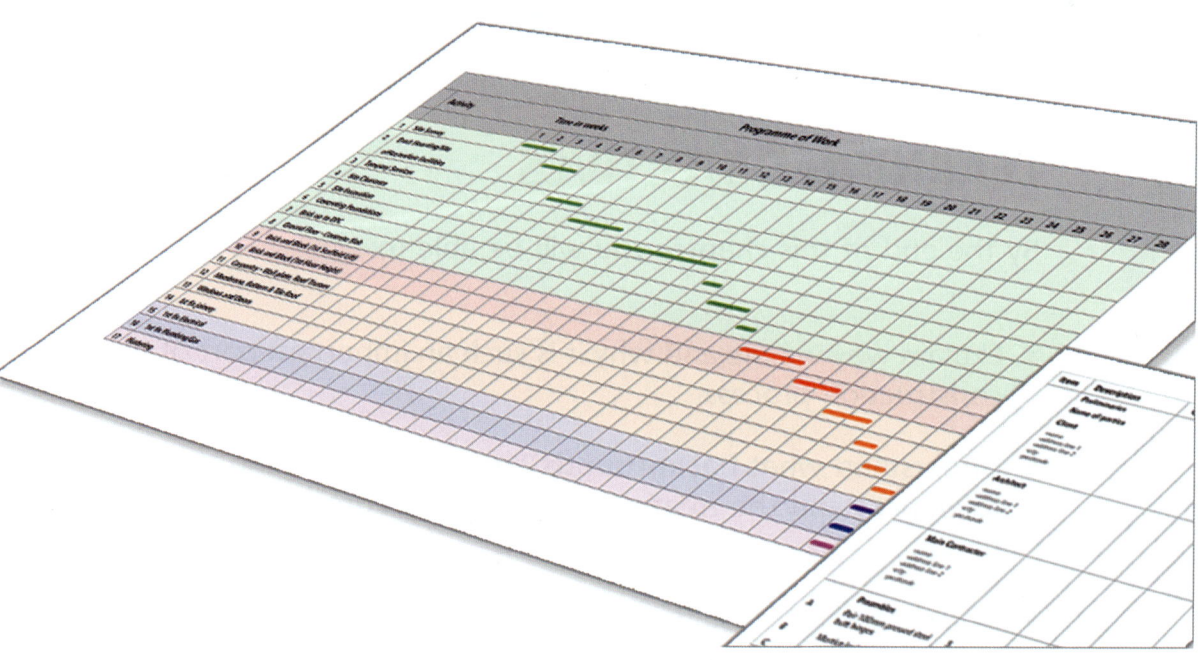

Example of work documents

Tiling is the process of laying tiles of different materials on walls and floors. The job includes being able to measure and set out areas for tiling then fix, cut and **grout** tiles.

Why we tile

Tiling is usually carried out to protect surfaces from water damage, e.g. in showers, the splashbacks around sinks and on bathroom and kitchen floors where there is heavy footfall and an easy, clean surface is desirable. It can also be used for decorative effect.

E-LEARNING

Use the e-learning programme to see an animated version of the advantages and disadvantages of tiling.

Advantages of tiling	Disadvantages of tiling
Protects surfaces. Extensive variety of colours and shapes available. Can be the most cost effective solution. Tiles are exceptionally durable as long as they are installed correctly. Certain tiles can be slip resistant, quieter than other flooring types and easily cleaned. If the building has **underfloor heating** you can have a warm tile floor.	Tiles are hard and if something breakable is dropped on the floor it is likely to be beyond repair. Tiles can be slippery if the appropriate tiles have not been selected for the area. Depending on the location of the building, tiled floors can be cold although this can be seen as an advantage in warmer areas. Consideration should also be given to the weight of floor tiles, particularly above the ground floor, and whether the floor can support the weight of the tiles.

Underfloor heating
A type of heating provided by water pipes or electric elements in the screed or electric mats on the floor screed under a floor. Underfloor heating can be used under tiled floors.

Skills required by a tiler

JOB VACANCY

Job Title: Tiler
Location: Nationwide
Hours: Average 37.5 hours per week
Work Pattern: Monday to Friday

Skills Required:
- Fit and healthy
- Practical ability
- Hand-eye co-ordination
- Attention to detail
- Numeracy skills
- Part of a team
- Artistic ability
- Working safely

NOTE ON UK STANDARDS

It is possible to train as a tiler at any age. Most people train on the job as well as attending a college or training centre to gain qualifications or train through a Modern Apprenticeship or Construction Apprenticeship.

Building design

Each building job will have a design specification document and a bill of quantities which will contain:

- Detailed plans of the build.
- Information on how the construction should be built.
- A list of materials that need to be used and their quantities.

GETTING STARTED

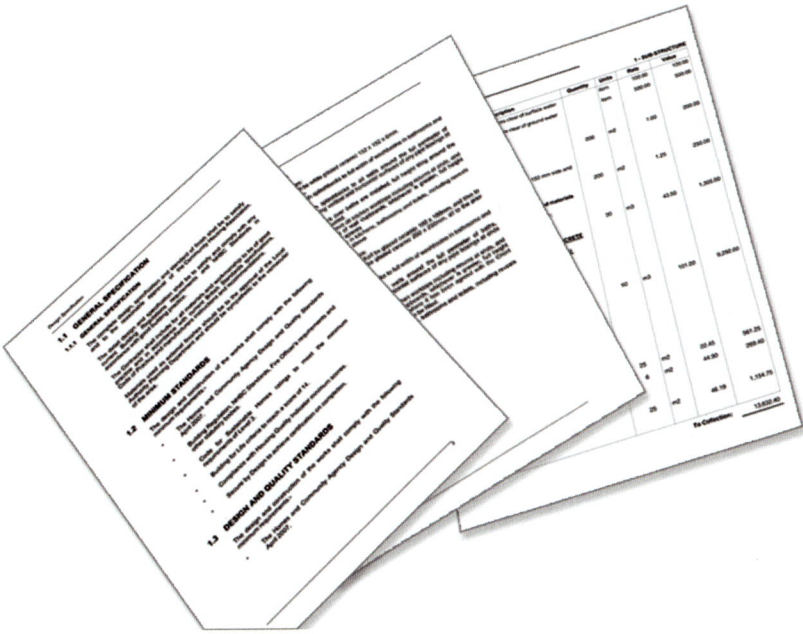

Design specifications and bill of quantities

NOTE ON UK STANDARDS

Design specification documents will be required to satisfy and comply with building regulations and meet the approval of local authorities. You will need to refer to and understand these documents to make sure the building is constructed correctly.

Scale drawings

It would be impractical to produce building drawings to their full size so they are reduced to a ratio of the real size, known as a scale drawing. For example, in a drawing to a scale of 1:10, 100mm will represent 1000mm or 1m, and on a scale 1:100, 100mm will represent 10,000mm or 10m. This means in order to calculate the actual measurement from the scale drawing you multiply the scale measurement by the scale ratio.

NOTE ON UK STANDARDS

All construction drawings are produced in accordance with British Standard 1192 Drawing Office Practice.

CONSTRUCTION: WALL AND FLOOR TILING

ACTIVITY

What measurement would 100mm represent in each of the following scales? Enter the values below.

1:2500 –

1:500 –

1:200 –

1:20 –

BACKGROUNDS

Types of background

Tiles can be fixed to a wide variety of surfaces, known as backgrounds, as long as they are properly prepared and the appropriate **adhesives** are used. The most common backgrounds are:

- aquapanel
- sand cement render
- plaster

Adhesive General term for a range of bonding agents.

GETTING STARTED

- plasterboard
- moisture board
- WBP (weather and boil proof) plywood
- sand cement floor screed
- underfloor heating mats.

Treatment of backgrounds

Tiling requires a perfectly flat background and preparation of the background is very important. Each background will require a different preparation.

Sand cement render

Sand cement **render** and sand cement **floor screeding** have similar methods as the surface dries gradually and shrinks as it dries. If this type of background is not cured and dried before tiling it can shrink, which can break the contact between the background and the tile adhesive, causing the tiling to fail. This applies to new or existing surfaces that have become saturated over time. Depending on the suction, or porosity of the render, a primer coat may be required before tiling begins.

> **Render** A sand and cement backing coat for tiling, usually applied in at least two coats.

> **Floor screed** The final layer of concrete laid on top of the oversite concrete to level off. The floor screed is usually laid later on in the project.

Sand cement render

CONSTRUCTION: WALL AND FLOOR TILING

Plaster

> **Plaster** A colourless, white or pinkish mineral formed from heating gypsum at high temperatures. Plaster is used to protect and enhance the appearance of a surface as it provides a joint-less finish.

Plaster must be thoroughly dry before tiling and should have been completed at least four weeks before tiling begins. If drying has been assisted by a space heater or dehumidifier, they must not be directed straight at the plasterwork and afterwards checks should be made to ensure that the plaster is not just dry at the surface.

The finished plaster should be specified in the design specification and applied to leave a matt finish. Tilers should first check that the surface is sound and that the layers of plaster have completely adhered. If the finished plaster has dusty residue on its surface it should be thoroughly brushed down and if the surface has become shiny and smooth this should be roughened by vigorous brushing. Tiles should always be applied to the plaster topcoat and not an undercoat.

Plaster

Plasterboard

> **Plasterboard** A type of board made of gypsum sandwiched between sheets of paper. It has a number of properties and can be made to different thicknesses and sizes for different areas and uses.

If tiling on **plasterboard**, it is essential that the joints have been taped, filled and smoothed, and that all dust from sanding has been removed before starting.

GETTING STARTED

Plasterboard

Moisture resistant plasterboard

Plasterboards can have moisture resistant properties for use in areas where moisture needs to be controlled such as bathrooms or kitchens, and generally have a green facing paper for easy identification. If you are applying a plaster skim to a moisture board then you should treat it with a **PVA** first.

> **PVA** The standard and widely used abbreviation for Polyvinyl Acetate.

Moisture resistant plasterboard

WBP

WBP or weather and boil proof plywood is an external grade of plywood which can withstand a certain amount of moisture due to the water repellent adhesive used in its construction. It can be used where an existing background is unsuitable for tiling, e.g. floorboards where there are many joints which may lead to excessive expansion and contraction. The WBP plywood is used to overboard the existing background and must be fixed with countersunk screws at a maximum of 300mm apart to provide a flat surface for tiling.

WBP

> **Keys** The preparation to backgrounds either chemically, mechanically, hacking or scratching before plaster or render is applied. Creating keys ensure that the plaster or render sticks and the method of keying will depend on the type of background.

Aquapanel

Aquapanel is a durable cement board that provides a suitable background for areas that will get wet, e.g. bathrooms and shower rooms, as it keeps its strength even when wet. Make sure the area you are installing the panels on to is dry before starting. Once installed you can begin tiling immediately as the board is already **keyed**.

Aquapanel

Underfloor heating mats

When tiling onto underfloor heating mats, ensure the adhesive fully covers the mat and that all the tiles are laid in close contact with the mat to gain maximum heat benefits.

Underfloor heating mat

CONSTRUCTION: WALL AND FLOOR TILING

ACTIVITY

Which types of background are terms that are new to you? Use a search engine to find out more about these backgrounds and write down where they are typically used.

Tolerances of backgrounds

E-LEARNING

Use the e-learning programme to see an animated version of checking the background.

Plumb The vertical level of a surface or structure.

Level The horizontal level of a surface or structure.

The background should be specified as 'to be tiled' in the design specification to ensure a **plumb**, true and **level** surface. This is essential as a plastered background that is not to be tiled is not required to meet the same tolerances.

GETTING STARTED 13

Ensure the surface is level and plumb

The background to be tiled should be checked with a 2m straightedge and a **spirit level**. A plumb, true and level background will not have any gaps between points of contact over 3mm.

Check for gaps

Spirit level A tool used to check true vertical and horizontal lines indicated by a bubble in spirit-filled vials.

14 CONSTRUCTION: WALL AND FLOOR TILING

There is a maximum weight that can be supported by different backgrounds which includes the weight of the tile, the adhesive and the grout. In all cases, you should follow the manufacturer's recommendations. Here are some approximate weight limits for a selection of backgrounds.

Aquapanel

Plasterboard

GETTING STARTED 15

WBP

ACTIVITY

Use a search engine to find out the weight of different ceramic wall tiles to cover a 1m² area of a bathroom wall. Which correctly prepared backgrounds will be able to support this weight?

CONSTRUCTION: WALL AND FLOOR TILING

COMMUNICATION

Communication with other trades

Although the tiler is not required on site until the second fix stage of the construction process, communication with other trades is very important. Backgrounds to be tiled need to be determined at the design specification stage to ensure that they meet the required standard and tolerance. This information will need to be passed to the bricklayer who may be laying concrete floors on the ground floor, the plasterer doing the walls and floors and possibly the underfloor heating contractors. The tiler will need to keep up to date with the progress of the project to allow drying times for backgrounds prior to tiling to ensure they are on site at the correct time.

Communicating with other people

ACTIVITY

List all the other trades or people you might need to communicate with when working on a project.

ACTIVITY

There are many methods of communicating information, how many can you think of and which would be classed as formal and which would be classed as informal?

CHECK YOUR KNOWLEDGE

1. **When checking the tolerance of a plastered background before tiling, what is the maximum permissible gap between points of contact over a distance of 2m?**

   ☐ a. 1mm

   ☐ b. 3mm

   ☐ c. 5mm

CONSTRUCTION: WALL AND FLOOR TILING

2. True or False: Tiling is a first fix trade.

☐ a. True

☐ b. False

3. True or False: A plasterboard background can support up to 50kg/m² of tiles.

☐ a. True

☐ b. False

4. List two types of formal communication that a tiler might use.

a.

b.

5. Fill in the blanks in this sentence:

The background should be specified as 'to be tiled' in the design specification to ensure a _____, _____ and _____ surface.

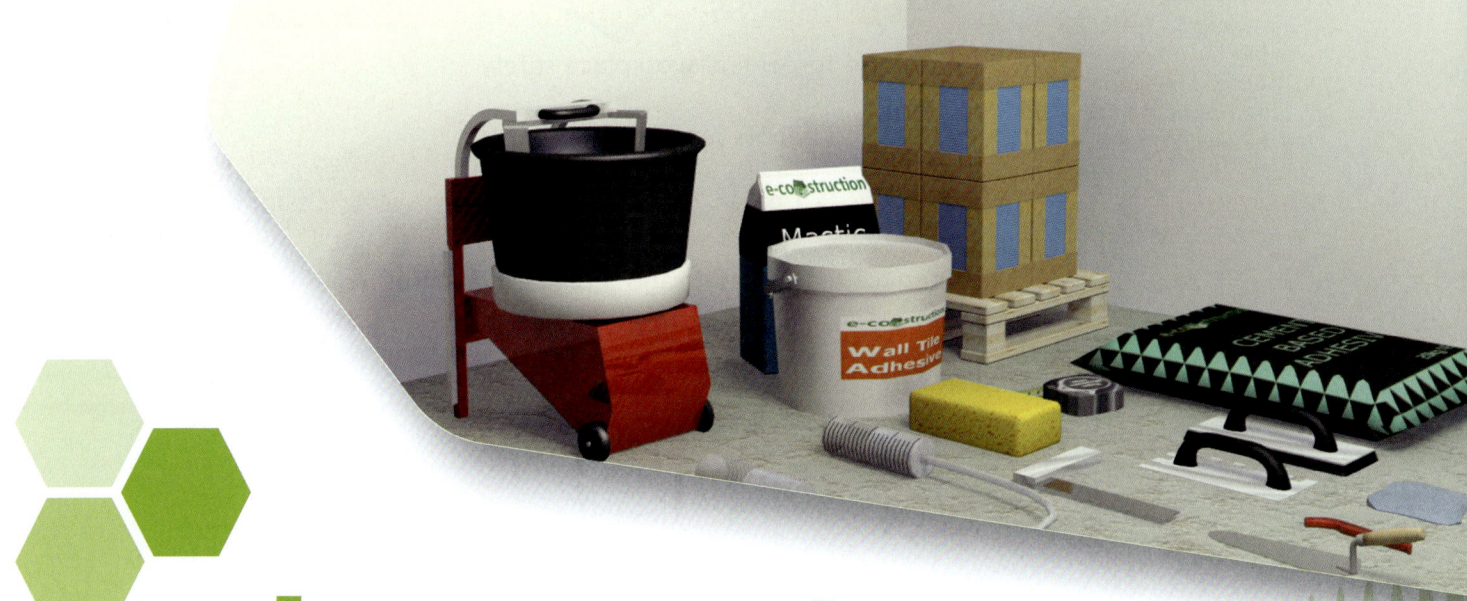

Chapter 2

MATERIALS

LEARNING OBJECTIVES

By the end of this chapter you will be able to:

- List the most common materials used in tiling.

- Identify the correct tools for work.

- Appreciate health, safety and welfare considerations.

- Understand risk assessment requirements.

- Identify **sustainable** sourcing and disposal methods.

- List the correct storage methods for materials.

CONSTRUCTION: WALL AND FLOOR TILING

Sustainable materials Materials that have been sourced by causing little or no damage to the environment.

NOS REFERENCE

Conform to general workplace safety

Move and handle resources

Tile wall and floor surfaces

Produce tiled, mosaic and stone surface finishes

Confirm work activities and resources for the work

TILES

Types of tiles

There are a wide range of tiles available and the selection will depend on where they are to be used, their properties and decorative value. Tile properties vary and it is important that the correct type of tile is chosen for the location to be tiled. As well as the tiles described here there are other types such as: glass, marble, granite, travertine and limestone. Some tiles need considerable expertise to lay them properly.

ACTIVITY

Match up the images of the tiles shown here with their correct names and descriptions.

Tile type	Description	Tiles
Glazed ceramic tiles	These tiles are made from natural clay and are most often found on floors. They come in a range of red and brown shades with a natural variation of colour but are not sealed so will change colour over time. The tiles have natural slip resistant properties and are very hard wearing.	

Glazed A ceramic coating in a glassy state or the material from which this coating is made.

MATERIALS 21

Tile type	Description	Tiles
Unglazed ceramic tiles	These tiles are the most common option for use on the walls of kitchens and bathrooms. They can also be used on the floors of conservatories and reception rooms. High quality tiles of this type can be an affordable option and can make a decorative impact with the varied sizes and colours available. However, they are not suitable for high traffic floor areas as they can be damaged by the grit brought in on shoes.	
Porcelain tiles	These tiles are natural stone tiles made from a mix of materials that has been compressed over millions of years. Some of them are very expensive and need considerable expertise to lay them properly. The tiles are hard wearing but need to be sealed as they can be quite porous. Guidance should be taken from the manufacturer as to their suitability for different locations.	
Quarry tiles	These tiles can be as small as $25mm^2$ and are usually supplied fixed to a $305mm^2$ fibreglass mesh sheet, which holds all of the tiles in place. This makes the tiles much easier and faster to lay as well as being ideal for tiling uneven areas or purposely curved walls.	
Mosaic tiles	These tiles can be quite robust and are ideal in high traffic areas such as laundries, utility rooms, playrooms and garages. They have slip resistant profiles which range from bare feet to shoes. The disadvantage of this type of tile is that the more slip resistant they are, the harder they are to clean.	

CONSTRUCTION: WALL AND FLOOR TILING

Tile type	Description	Tiles
Slate tiles	These are robust and good for high traffic areas; they can also be extremely attractive and can be produced to look like natural stone tiles. They are available for walls and floors and are fired at very high temperatures which makes them extremely hard wearing. They can also have anti slip properties.	

ACTIVITY

Which types of tiles are new to you? Use a search engine to find out more about these tiles and write down where they are typically used.

MATERIALS

Tiles sizes

> **E-LEARNING**
>
> Use the e-learning programme to see an animated version of different sized tiles in use.

Tiles range in size from the most common 150 × 150mm tiles to large 600 × 600mm tiles. A tile design may use the same size tile for the whole project or can include different sizes to create different looks. Tiles are usually supplied in boxes or packs to cover a predefined area.

Tile sizes can vary

Take precautions when lifting

CONSTRUCTION: WALL AND FLOOR TILING

HEALTH & SAFETY

The tiler should use correct manual handling techniques when lifting any tiles and should not lift anything above 25kg on his/her own.

ADHESIVES AND GROUT

Tile adhesives

Tiles are fixed to the background by the use of a tile adhesive and there are a large number of adhesives available, both ready mixed and as cement based adhesives that are mixed as required. The type of adhesive will depend on the tiles being used and location being tiled, but it is essential that the correct adhesive is used if the tiling is to last, e.g. the adhesive may need to be heat resistant or waterproof.

If the adhesive needs to be mixed, the proportions will be given on the packaging and stirring with a mechanical mixer for at least 5 minutes will ensure a usable mix. Ambient temperatures below 5°C and above 30°C will affect the setting time of tile adhesives and can make them impossible to use.

Have your materials all ready

ACTIVITY

Use a search engine to find out more about the different types of tile adhesives and list them here along with their main uses.

Mastic

Mastic adhesives provide an alternative to traditional tile adhesives and can be quicker to use on vertical surfaces due to the higher initial 'grab' of the tile. They do, however, have some limitations including they are only suitable for internal, thin bed applications of up to 2mm and are also not suitable for floor tiles or particularly dense tiles.

> **Mastic adhesive** An alternate adhesive suitable for tiling walls as it has a quicker initial 'grab'. The limitation of mastic adhesive is that it is only suitable for thin bed application which makes it unsuitable for tiling floors.

Grouts

Once tiles have been fixed to the background and left to dry for at least 12 hours, the spaces between the tiles are then filled with grout. Grouts are available in a range of colours and can have a significant impact on the overall appearance of a tiled surface.

Depending on the tiles used and the location they are being used in, the correct grout is essential, e.g. it may may need water resistant properties. Coloured grouts have a small risk of staining the tiles they are being used on so a small test should be carried out and if staining is a risk, the surface should be sealed prior to grouting. Grouts should not be used when the ambient temperature is below 5°C as this can cause the grout to discolour.

CONSTRUCTION: WALL AND FLOOR TILING

Use the correct grout for the situation

HEALTH & SAFETY

Tile adhesives and grouts present a number of hazards to the tiler due to the compounds they contain:

- Skin irritation can be avoided by the use of gloves.
- Goggles should be worn if working above eye level to prevent any adhesive or grout falling into the eyes.
- The area being tiled should be well ventilated and if necessary a dust mask should be worn to prevent inhalation of the adhesive or grout.
- Kneepads should be worn when tiling floors to prevent physical damage to the knees and also to prevent any adhesive or grout on the clothes making contact with the skin.

PPE should be worn where necessary

ACTIVITY

Can you draw some of the health and safety signs you may see on a building site?

a. Safety gloves must be worn.

b. Safety goggles or glasses must be worn.

c. Dust mask must be worn.

d. First-aid point located here.

SPACERS AND TRIMS

Tile spacers

Tile spacers are usually small pieces of cross-shaped plastic that fit between the tiles as they are being laid to ensure an even

> **Tile spacers** Small plastic shapes that fit between the tiles as they are being laid to ensure an even professional finish. They are available in a number of different sizes and the size required will depend on the size of tile being used.

Tile spacers can be used in different configurations

CONSTRUCTION: WALL AND FLOOR TILING

professional finish. They are available in a number of different sizes and the size required will depend on the size of tile being used.

Trims

> **E-LEARNING**
>
> Use the e-learning programme to see an animated version of applying a tile trim.

Tile trim Edgings that protect the edges of tiles that meet at 90° and also create a professional finish. They are used on internal and external corners.

Tile trims are used to protect the edges of tiles that meet at 90° and also to create a professional finish on internal and external corners and tiled panels.

The trim is fixed to the wall with tile adhesive although it can also be tacked temporarily until the tiles have reached a high enough point to hold the trim in place.

When the adhesive holding the trim has set, tiles can be fixed to the wall covering the edge of the trim.

Fix the trim in place

Apply adhesive to the area

Tile over the trim

CONSTRUCTION: WALL AND FLOOR TILING

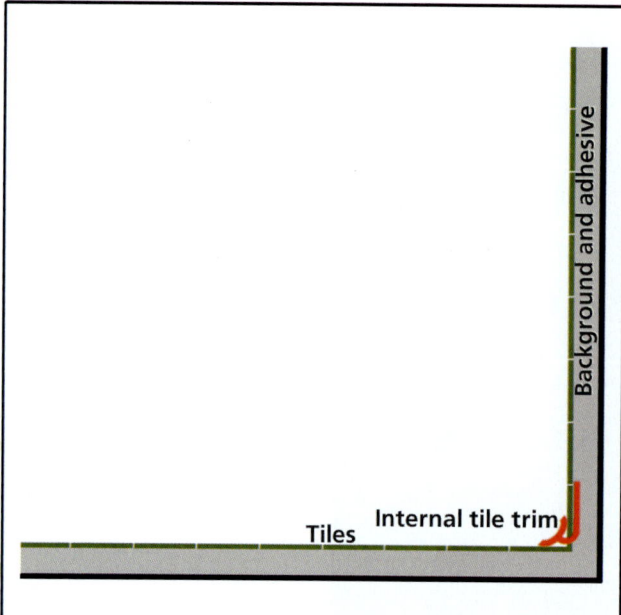

Positioning of an internal angle trim

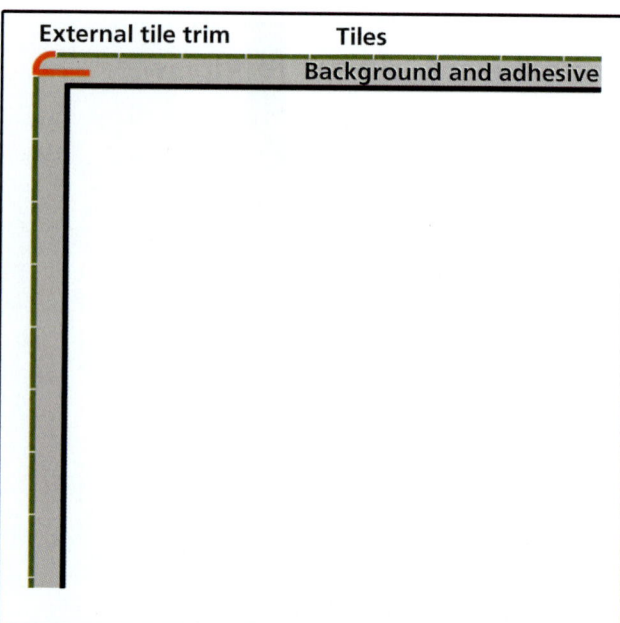

Positioning of an external angle trim

TOOLS

Tools for setting out

There are a number of tools used in the **setting out** process when preparing to tile a wall or floor. Here are some of the most common ones.

> **Setting out** The process of planning how the tiles are going to be laid out on a surface. It includes measuring your surface areas, checking the laying of tiles, planning the tile order and making sure everything is plumb and level.

E-LEARNING

Use the e-learning programme to view the tools for setting out information in a flip book.

Spirit level

A spirit level is used to check that the background and the completed tiling are level.

Spirit level

Laser levels

A line **laser level** puts out a single line across a wall or surface whereas a dual-beam sends a beam vertically and horizontally. Rotary levels are normally mounted on a tripod and run a line all the way around a room.

Laser level A mechanical device mounted on a stand which extends to the height of the room. The laser level projects the horizontal and vertical levels on to the surface using laser beams.

Laser level

Water level

A **water level** is simpler and cheaper than other levels. It works on the principle that water finds its own level and is useful for findings levels on different walls in different rooms.

Water level A tool used for transferring levels from one wall or room to another. This tool consists of two plastic water containers, tubing filled with water and an air release valve on a gauge rod. The same level on the walls in two different rooms can be achieved by matching the water level of each of the water containers to the same level.

CONSTRUCTION: WALL AND FLOOR TILING

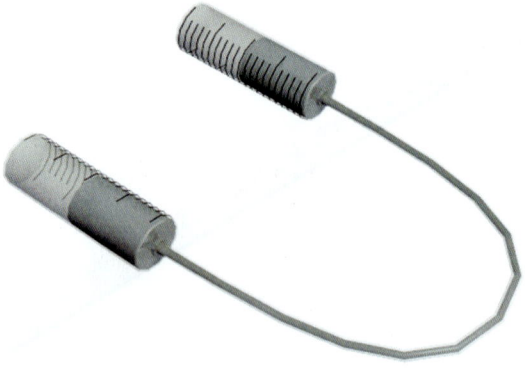

Water level

Batten

Batten (tiling) Timber strip fixed to the wall to support the first course of whole tiles.

A horizontal **batten** is fixed under the line of the first row of whole tiles from the floor whereas a vertical batten is fixed next to the last vertical line of whole tiles from the wall.

Batten

Ruler and tape measure

A ruler or tape measure is used to measure the area to be tiled and also to mark cuts on tiles.

MATERIALS 33

Tape measure

Gauge stick

A **gauge stick** is a wooden batten with marks to show the line of each join between tiles, including the spaces between tiles. It is used to mark out vertical guidelines for laying tiles. Guidelines should be marked at 1m intervals around the room and a spirit level should be used to check the marks are vertical.

> **Gauge stick** A timber batten marked with tile size measurements to help establish the most acceptable setting out on each wall.

Gauge stick

Set square

A **set square** can be used to mark square cuts on tiles and for marking out floor areas.

> **Set square** A tool used for marking or checking right angle lines.

CONSTRUCTION: WALL AND FLOOR TILING

Set square

Chalk line

A **chalk line** is used to mark straight lines on wall and floor surfaces.

Chalk line A length of string, coated in chalk dust, which is used to produce accurate straight lines. The line is held at both ends and snapped against a surface thus transferring chalk dust to it.

Chalk line

ACTIVITY

Find the following setting out tools in the wordsearch below.

G	A	U	G	E	S	T	I	C	K	L	P	I
E	R	A	U	Q	S	T	E	S	R	Y	L	E
L	E	K	J	D	K	X	X	E	N	P	P	A
S	A	W	A	T	E	R	L	E	V	E	L	N
G	E	S	U	K	I	U	T	Y	G	P	S	K
X	U	Q	E	E	R	T	S	S	Y	J	W	A
D	O	L	R	R	A	F	O	N	Z	W	M	M
A	C	O	U	B	L	A	C	P	Z	Z	M	M
P	E	R	U	S	A	E	M	E	P	A	T	S
W	F	L	F	J	H	B	V	D	S	R	K	R
P	I	R	J	E	L	L	C	E	F	D	Q	X
C	H	A	L	K	L	I	N	E	L	M	O	S
S	P	I	R	I	T	L	E	V	E	L	L	J

BATTEN, SET SQUARE, CHALK LINE, SPIRIT LEVEL, GAUGE STICK, TAPE MEASURE, LASER LEVEL, WATER LEVEL, RULER

Tools for tiles

There are a number of tools used when cutting and fixing tiles. Here are some of the most common ones.

E-LEARNING

Use the e-learning programme to view the tools for cutting tiles in a flip book.

Tile cutter

To use a tile cutter, cut marks are lined up with the cutting wheel which is then moved across the tile to score the surface. The tile is then snapped in the jaws of the cutter.

Tile cutter

Nibblers and tile file

Nibblers are used to remove small amounts from the edge of a tile which is smoothed with a **tile file** afterwards.

Nibbler A hand tool used to cut tiles by making a series of small cuts to achieve a particular shape or size. After cutting, a tile file should be used to smooth the edges.

Tile file A tool used to smooth off edges after a tile has been cut.

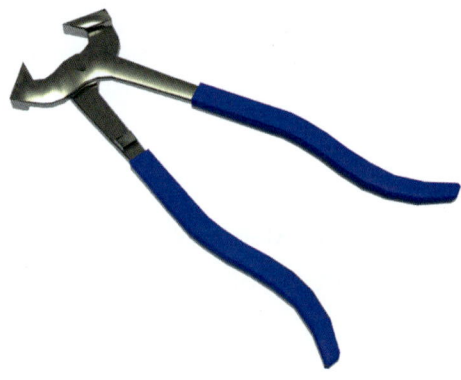

Tile nibbler

Tile scorer

A **tile scorer** is used to score the tile along the cutting mark; the tile is then snapped across a batten. It can also be used for irregular shapes.

Tile scorer A tool with a needle used to score a mark on the face of a tile. The tile can then be snapped across a wooden batten.

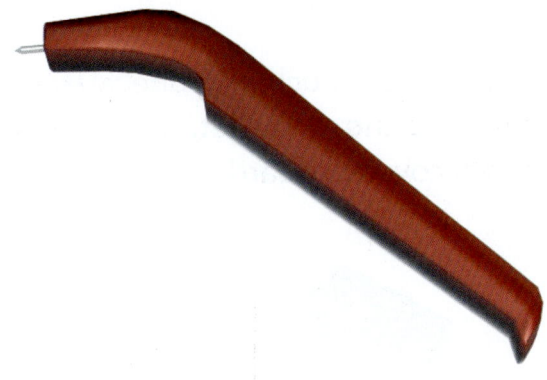
Tile scorer

Wet saw

A **wet saw** can be used to cut various types of tiles including thicker tiles such as quarry tiles.

> **Wet saw** A tool used for cutting thicker tiles. This saw has a motorized circular blade which cuts through the tile whilst being splashed with water.

Wet saw

Rod saw

A rod saw is a small lightweight tool that can cut a variety of materials. It is useful for cutting curves or awkward shapes.

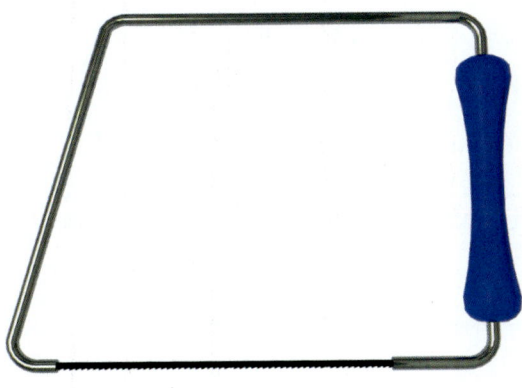
Rod saw

CONSTRUCTION: WALL AND FLOOR TILING

Mallet

A mallet is used to bed tiles such as stone, slate and mosaic into the adhesive. Before using a mallet, the tiles should be protected with a carpet covered board.

Mallet

Find the following tile tools in the wordsearch below.

P	T	I	L	E	F	I	L	E	W	R
I	R	E	R	O	C	S	E	L	I	T
A	T	I	L	E	C	U	T	T	E	R
R	Y	X	U	T	S	P	N	E	D	O
S	U	I	V	E	R	R	N	W	R	M
R	P	N	X	L	E	O	I	E	K	M
K	M	D	U	L	L	D	M	T	G	D
T	J	V	M	A	B	S	K	S	O	T
A	G	L	H	M	B	A	X	A	V	I
W	I	K	U	C	I	W	Y	W	R	I
L	B	Y	F	L	N	V	T	I	M	V

MALLET, TILE FILE, NIBBLERS, TILE SCORER, ROD SAW, WET SAW, TILE CUTTER

MATERIALS 39

> **E-LEARNING**
>
> Use the e-learning programme to view the tools for adhesives information in a flip book.

Tools for adhesives

There are two main tools used with adhesives.

Gauging trowel

A **gauging trowel** is normally used to scoop the adhesive from the tub or container on to the notched trowel where it is then applied to the background.

> **Gauging trowel** A popular trowel used for the mixing, bedding and placing of materials.

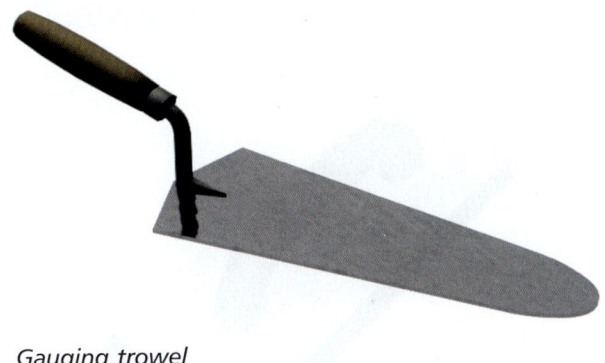

Gauging trowel

Notched trowel

A **notched trowel** is designed to spread the adhesive on to a background. The size of the trowel will depend on the tiles and adhesive being used.

> **Notched trowel** A trowel used for the even application of adhesives to walls and floors. Notches come in different size and shapes and the correct notched trowel to use will depend on the tile being fixed.

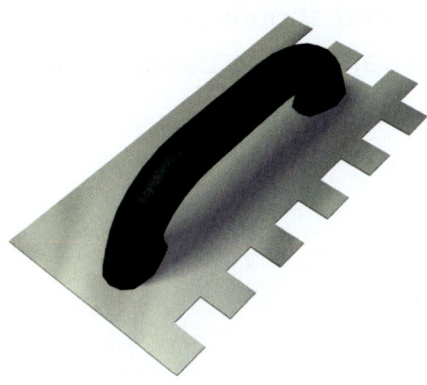

Notched trowel

CONSTRUCTION: WALL AND FLOOR TILING

Tools for grouting

The final stage of tiling is grouting. Here are some of the most common tools used to carry out this process.

E-LEARNING

Use the e-learning programme to view the tools for grouting information in a flip book.

Grout float

Grout is placed on the **float**, not the tiles; it is then used to spread the grout across the tiles and into the joints. Excess grout is removed with a clean float held at 45°.

> **Float** A range of tools which can be made from a variety of materials with a grip that holds a thin flat base approximately 100mm × 250mm. There are a number of different floats for different purposes including plasterer's float, devil float and grout float.

> **Grout float** A float with a rubber base used for grouting floor and wall tiles. The grout is placed on the grout float and not on the surface when applying.

> **Grout sponge** A sponge with rounded edges for removing excess grout on tiles during grouting.

Grout float

Grout sponge

A damp **grout sponge** is used to remove the excess grout from the face of the tiles and should always be used in the direction of the joints. It must always be dampened with clean water.

Grout sponge

Grout finisher

A **grout finisher** is used to smooth the grout for an even finish and can also be used on sealant.

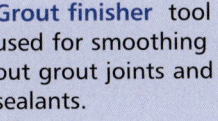

Grout finisher tool used for smoothing out grout joints and sealants.

Grout finisher

Dry cloth

After the grout has dried, usually the following day, a dry, soft and clean cloth is used to polish off any remaining powdery film.

Dry cloth

42 CONSTRUCTION: WALL AND FLOOR TILING

Grout remover

> **Grout remover** A tool used for removing old grouts before re-grouting during renovation projects.

Grout remover is used to remove the grout between tiles before they are re-grouted and is ideal for renovation projects.

Grout remover

Sealant

> **Sealant** A filler that is used for covering joints in tiles where grouting is not suitable. For example, corners, sinks, baths and other wet areas.

Sealant can be used to seal internal corners where grouting is not possible; this provides extra protection against water damage. Sealant is usually used to seal edges around baths, sinks, showers and other wet areas.

Sealant

ACTIVITY

Find the following grouting tools in the wordsearch below.

D	A	I	B	S	V	M	W	V	B	R	C	G
W	O	U	P	E	M	E	H	L	R	G	J	R
X	A	J	M	A	S	L	A	Q	E	R	W	O
G	R	D	Z	L	V	Y	Z	Q	V	O	R	U
R	R	Y	M	A	L	S	H	Z	O	U	J	T
O	K	Z	M	N	R	A	T	J	M	T	F	F
U	R	Z	N	T	T	P	O	L	E	S	I	I
T	N	Y	O	I	S	A	L	R	R	P	I	N
F	H	F	F	X	I	H	C	R	T	O	I	I
L	Y	O	G	E	I	P	Y	V	U	N	K	S
O	L	O	A	Y	V	Z	R	P	O	G	G	H
A	O	D	X	B	R	C	D	L	R	E	R	E
T	E	H	T	N	L	Z	W	J	G	U	K	R

DRY CLOTH, GROUT REMOVER, GROUT FINISHER, GROUT SPONGE, GROUT FLOAT, SEALANT

ORDERING MATERIALS

Calculating material quantities

When calculating the quantity of tiles required you will need to first work out the surface area required to be tiled. To do this multiply the width and height of each individual area that is to be tiled and add them together.

The box containing your tiles will tell you the design specification of the tiles. This includes the number of tiles contained in the box and the amount of surface area they will approximately cover. Your tile supplier should also be able to give you this information.

CONSTRUCTION: WALL AND FLOOR TILING

> **E-LEARNING**
>
> Use the e-learning programme to see an animated version of the materials calculation.

FUNCTIONAL SKILLS

Take a room with a total surface area of 9.84m². It is to be tiled using 150 × 150mm tiles that come in a box of 44 and cover approximately 1m².	
To work out the number of boxes of tiles required, divide the total surface area of the room to be tiled by the coverage of a box.	9.84m²/1m² = 9.84 boxes of tiles.
Add 10 per cent wastage.	9.84 + 0.984 = 10.824 boxes of tiles which is rounded up to 11 boxes.

Once you have calculated the area to be tiled and the number of tiles required, you then need to order the correct amount of adhesive and grout.

ACTIVITY

FUNCTIONAL SKILLS

In most cases, 10 litres of adhesive will cover approximately 7m² of tiles and 3.5kg of grout will cover approximately 8m², based on 150 × 150mm tiles with a 2mm joint.

Using these values, how much adhesive and grout would you need to order to tile a room with a total surface area of 9.84m²?

Show your working out below.

MATERIALS 45

ACTIVITY

How many different ways of ordering materials can you think of? List your answers below.

MATERIALS ORDER FORM		
Order No:		**Date:**
Site Address:		
Site Name/Address of Supplier:		
Please supply the following order to the above address:		
Description:	**Quantity:**	**Date Required:**
Special Delivery Instructions:		
Signature of Site Manager:		

Example of an ordering form

Sourcing materials

SUSTAINABILITY

Ordering building materials from local suppliers contributes to lower carbon emission levels by reducing the carbon miles involved in transporting the materials; you may also save on packaging and shipping costs. Depending on the build, buying from a local independent business means you can benefit from local knowledge and expertise.

Apparent cost savings from long-distance suppliers can be lost if a delivery fails to arrive on time or arrives damaged or incomplete. This could cause major delays for a project and add pressure to your budget.

Think of your carbon footprint when sourcing materials

ACTIVITY

How would you find out about your local suppliers? Use the methods you find out about to make a list of local suppliers and what they can be used for.

STORAGE OF MATERIALS

Storing tiles

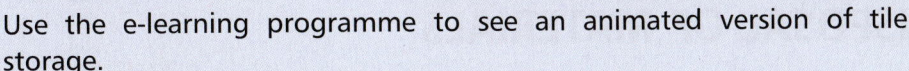

E-LEARNING

Use the e-learning programme to see an animated version of tile storage.

For safety and efficiency, materials should be stored properly. Tiles are a very fragile product and need to be stored in an area where they are unlikely to be struck by anything else. They can be stored flat or on their sides but in either case they should be raised off the ground. Tiles stored on their sides should be prevented from falling over.

Tiles should be left in their original packaging until they are needed to prevent them getting dirty or wet. If they are covered with a tarpaulin they can safely be stored outside but if they are, they should be allowed to acclimatize to room temperature before they are laid to prevent them cracking. Packs should be moved carefully to prevent damage to the tiles.

Tiles should be stored in the correct conditions

HEALTH & SAFETY

The tiler should use correct manual handling techniques when lifting any tiles and should not lift anything above 25kg on his/her own.

DISPOSAL OF MATERIALS

Landfill

SUSTAINABILITY

The UK construction industry produces over 36,000,000 tonnes of landfill waste every year. Sources of waste vary depending on the phase of construction, the method and the type of building but most waste is produced through over ordering, damage by mishandling, inadequate storage or the weather. Unnecessary packaging of construction materials also contributes a large amount of waste as plastic and cardboard.

Waste minimization strategies

SUSTAINABILITY

There are three basic ways of dealing with waste: Reduce, Reuse, Recycle.

Preventing waste in the first place is the ideal solution and this can be achieved by identifying possible waste streams early on in the build process. It is estimated that over ordering leads to 13,000,000 tonnes of new building materials being wasted every year. Improved communication between everyone involved in a build can ensure exact calculations of required materials are made and that unnecessary waste is prevented. Carefully timed deliveries can help to reduce waste caused by inadequate storage and damage.

Once waste has been created, one solution to managing it is to reuse it. Many materials can be reclaimed and possibly sold to offset the costs of a building project. For example, good quality tiles or tiles of historic interest removed from a renovation project can be sold to architectural salvage companies.

Recycling is another option for managing waste. Materials that can be recycled need to be identified early in the build process and separated from the other materials for easy storage, collection and transfer. An effective recycling strategy needs links to established local recycling facilities and contractors. Use of recycled materials on site can reduce cost and second-hand tiles are available from architectural salvage dealers. These can be used as part of the design effect, either on their own or mixed with new tiles.

ACTIVITY

Research the different ways in which tiles and other materials can be recycled, and list your findings here.

WEBLINKS

ACTIVITY

Use a search engine or any other method you can think of to find out about any local architectural salvage dealers or places where you can take your materials to be disposed of sustainably and list them here. You may even be able to source materials from these places. Make a note of their details here.

CHECK YOUR KNOWLEDGE

1. **What health and safety equipment is recommended when using tile adhesives and grouts?**

   ☐ a. Fire extinguisher

   ☐ b. Gloves

   ☐ c. Goggles

   ☐ d. Hard hat

   ☐ e. Knee pads

   ☐ f. Dust mask

2. How many boxes of 200 × 250mm tiles do you need to cover an area of 4m² with 10 per cent wastage?

   (Note: one box of 25, 200 × 250mm tiles covers an area of 1.25m².)

3. True or False: Tiles that have been stored outside can be used immediately.

   ☐ a. True
   ☐ b. False

4. List four tools that can be used when grouting tiles.

   1.
   2.
   3.
   4.

5. Fill in the blanks in the following sentence

   Waste minimization strategies include R_____, R_____ and R_____

Chapter 3

SETTING OUT

LEARNING OBJECTIVES

By the end of this chapter you will be able to:

- Explain how to set out a wall or floor for tiling.

- Explain how and why different tools are used to establish a level for tiling.

CONSTRUCTION: WALL AND FLOOR TILING

NOS REFERENCE

Tile wall and floor surfaces

Produce tiled, mosaic and stone surface finishes

Provide drainage for tiled surfaces

SETTING OUT FLOOR TILES

Marking out a floor

E-LEARNING

Use the e-learning programme to see an animated explanation of setting out floor tiles.

Tiled floors look best when the tiles are centred either in the middle of the room or with the centre line of the doorway. To begin marking out your floor:

1. Mark the centre point on the two shortest walls and use a chalk line to mark the line between these two points.

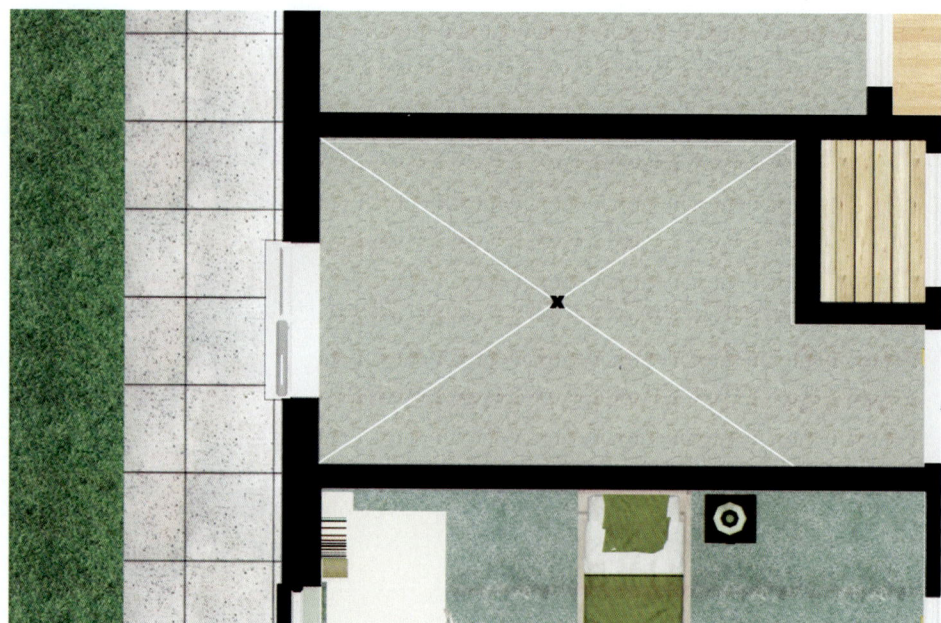

Finding the centre line (line 1)

2. You now have a centre line across the longest length of the room which is referred to as line 1.

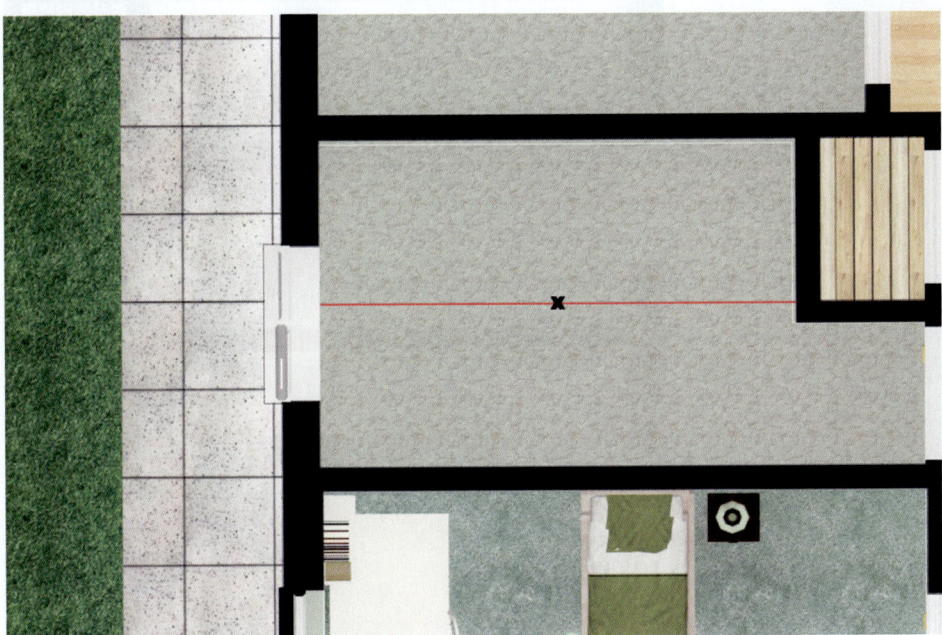

Marking the centre line

3. Find either the centre point of line 1 or the centre point of the door into the room on line 1.
4. To ensure your second line is exactly 90° to line 1, place a compass at the centre of line 1 and mark 2 points on line 1 at equal distances from the centre.
5. Place the compass on each of these two points and mark a line at approximately 90° to line 1 on both sides.

CONSTRUCTION: WALL AND FLOOR TILING

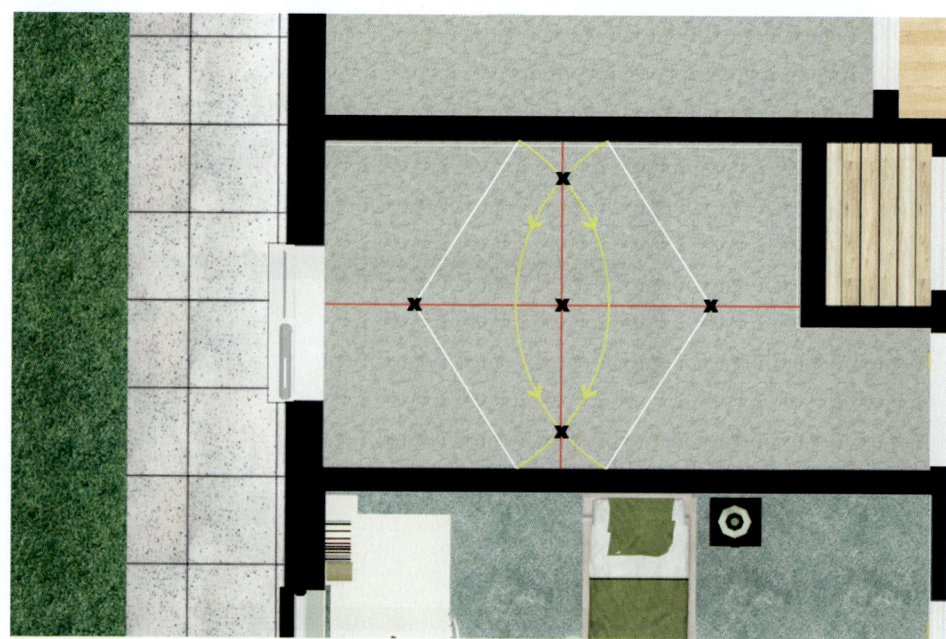

Ensuring line 2 is at 90 degrees

6. Where these marks cross gives you the position of your second line. Use another chalk line to mark this line which is referred to as line 2.

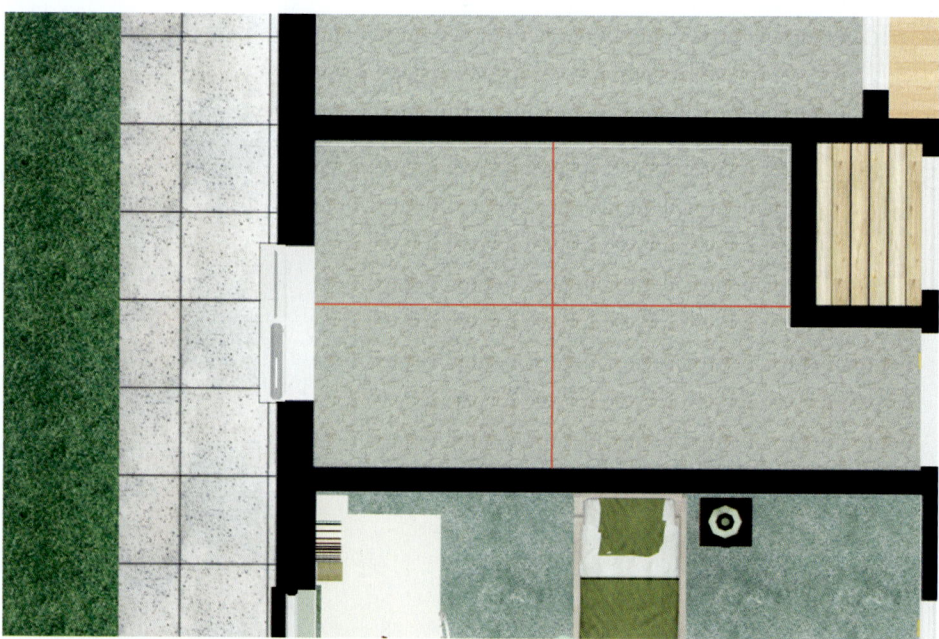

Marking line 2

ACTIVITY

Mark lines 1 and 2 on the floor plan below using a pencil, ruler and compass.

Checking the lines

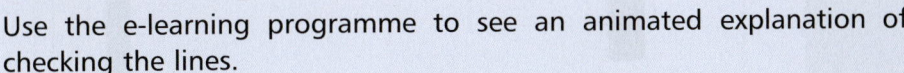

E-LEARNING

Use the e-learning programme to see an animated explanation of checking the lines.

Once you have marked the centre lines on a floor:

1. Dry lay one line of tiles along both these lines using the correct tile spacers to ensure you leave space for the grouting until you have laid the last whole tile.

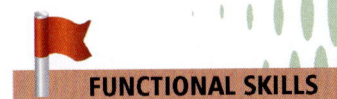

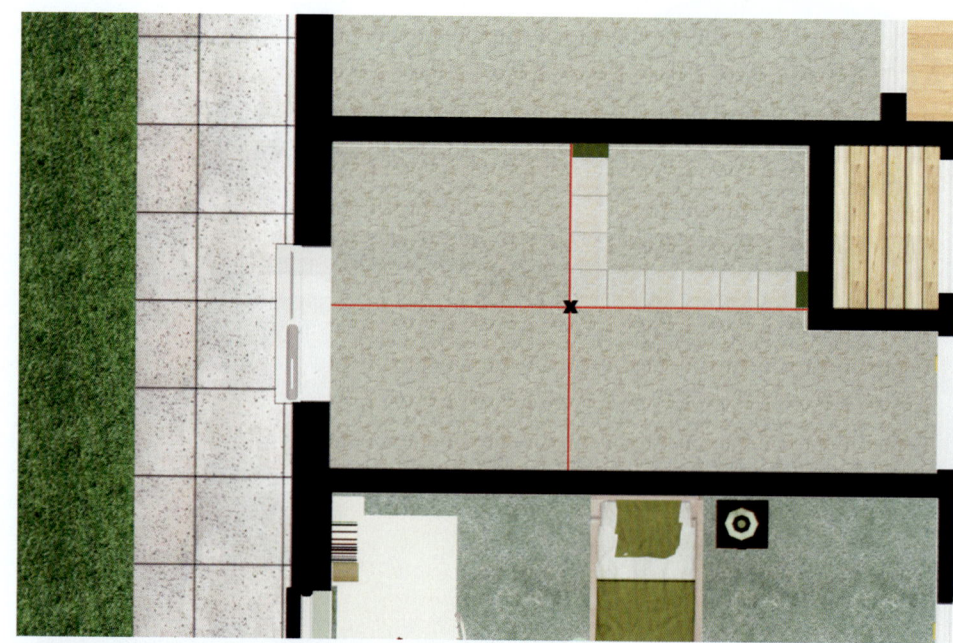

Checking the tile positions

2. Check the spacing around the edge of the room and if the last tile would be less than half a tile you will need to adjust the tiles or the lines.

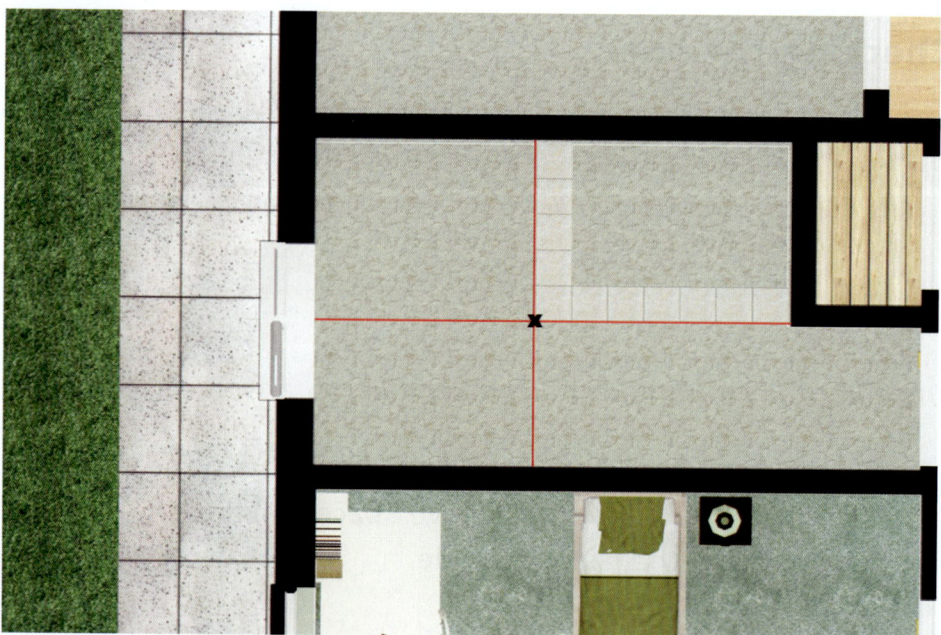

Move the centre lines if necessary

3. If you adjust the tiles then you must mark a new line to work with.

Shower and wet room floors

The majority of floors when tiled need to be flat. However, a wet room or shower floor will need to slope to allow the water to run to the drain. There should be a fall of at least 75mm from the each corner of the room to the drain to ensure the water drains efficiently.

Tiling should begin after all pipework has been installed. Start at the drain and work outwards using whole tiles as often as possible. Once the adhesive and grout is dry, the drain assembly should be adjusted so that it sits flush with the tiles and can then be sealed.

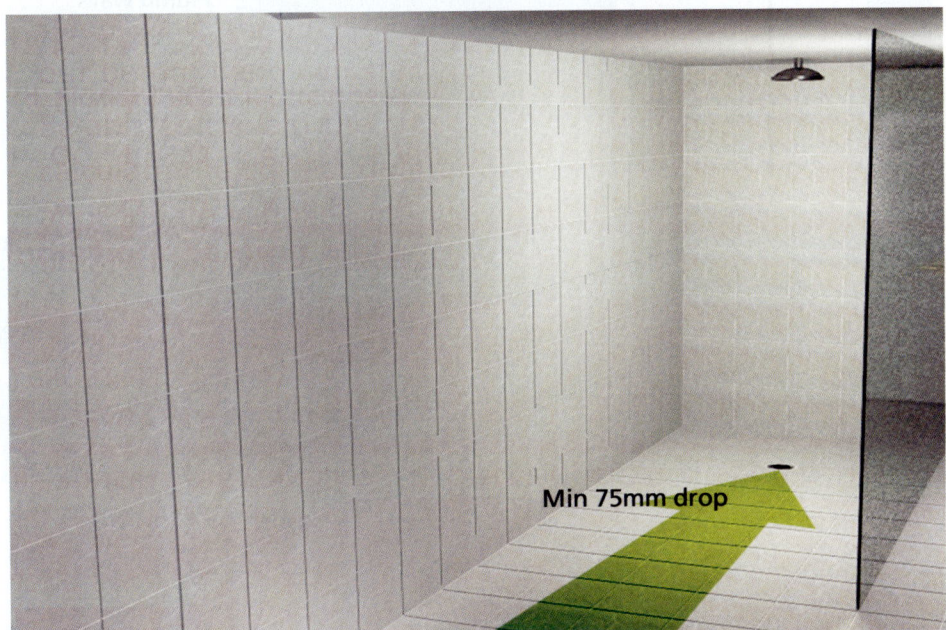

Floor measurements must be accurate

SETTING OUT WALL TILES

Considerations

Before beginning any wall tiling, there are a number of things that need to be taken into consideration:

- Where will the tiles fall in relation to the height and width of the wall?

- Will you be using a number of whole tiles or will there be cut tiles included?
- If you do need to cut tiles, where will these cuts fall?
- Are the ceiling and floor level, and the walls plumb?
- Are there any focal points such as windows to consider?

Plan your tiling carefully

Marking out plain walls

For whole, plain walls you will need to mark out the horizontal and vertical guides.

E-LEARNING

Use the e-learning programme to see an animated explanation of marking out plain walls.

ACTIVITY

How do you think you would mark out the horizontal guides for a plain wall? Number the following tasks in their correct order and then order the figures as well.

Order	Task	Order	Figure
	Fix a batten along the line. This will be the base from which you start tiling.		(room with diagonal X lines and horizontal red line)
	Measure the height of the wall and mark a horizontal centre line across the wall.		(room with vertical measure and horizontal red line)
	Check this line is straight using a spirit, laser or water level.		(room with vertical measure, horizontal red line and up/down arrows)

FUNCTIONAL SKILLS

Order	Task	Order	Figure
	If the bottom tile works out to be a cut tile of less than half a tile height, you will need to move the centre line up or down by half a tile and then repeat the process.		
	From this line, use your tile gauge and mark the position of the tiles down to the floor level.		
	Draw a line across the wall at the bottom of the lowest row of whole tiles.		

ACTIVITY

How do you think you would mark out the vertical guides for a plain wall? Number the following tasks in their correct order and then order the figures as well.

Order	Task	Order	Figure
	Mark out the vertical rows of tiles using your tile gauge until you reach the point at which the last whole tile falls.		
	Attach a vertical batten at this point.		
	Mark the centre of the wall.		
	Use a level to ensure this line is plumb.		

CONSTRUCTION: WALL AND FLOOR TILING

ACTIVITY

This diagram is drawn at a 1:20 scale. If you are tiling the facing wall with 150mm × 150mm tiles, where would you fix your horizontal and vertical battens? Draw the battens on the diagram.

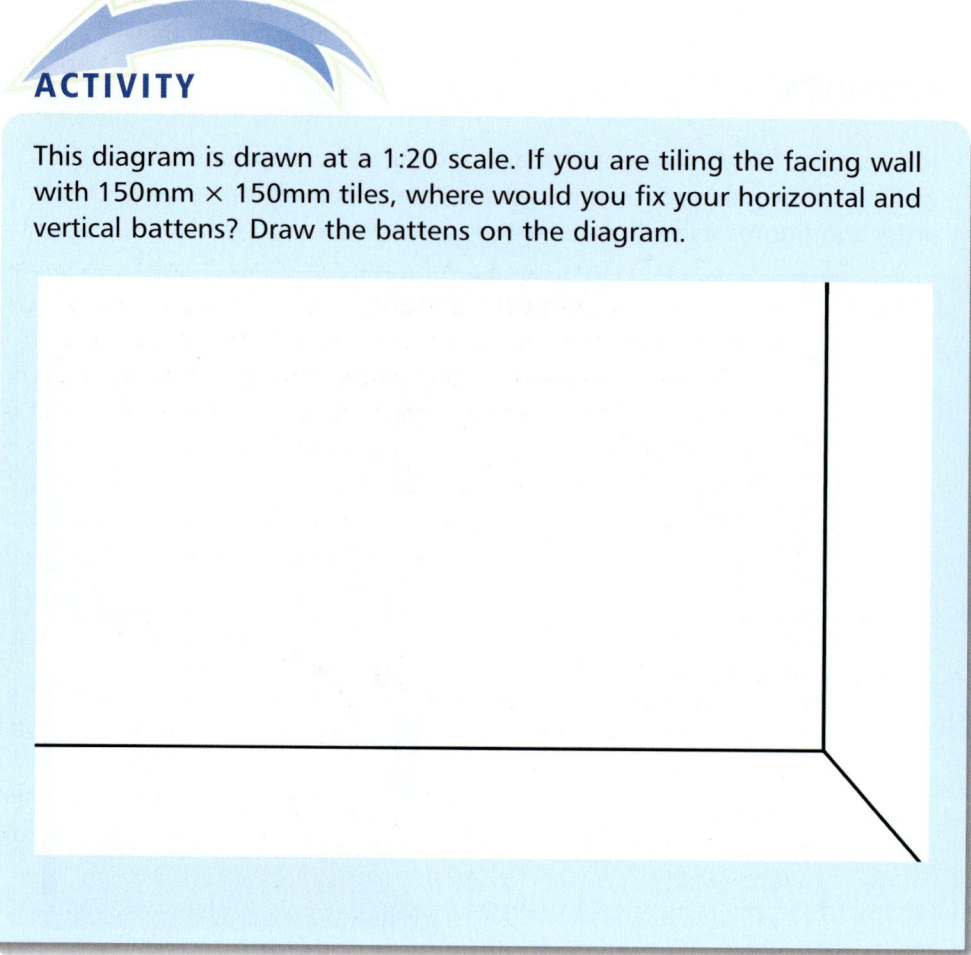

Marking out part-tiled walls

E-LEARNING

Use the e-learning programme to see an animated explanation of marking out part-tiled walls.

If you are only part-tiling a wall, you will need to consider the point at which the tiles stop, e.g. above a work surface or bath. For aesthetic reasons, when part-tiling a wall, it is better to have a whole tile at the top and also a whole tile at the bottom, if this is practical. If it is not practical to have a whole tile at the bottom, a line should be marked at the bottom of the lowest row of whole tiles and a batten fixed at this point. Vertical marking is then carried out in the same way as for a plain wall.

SETTING OUT | 65

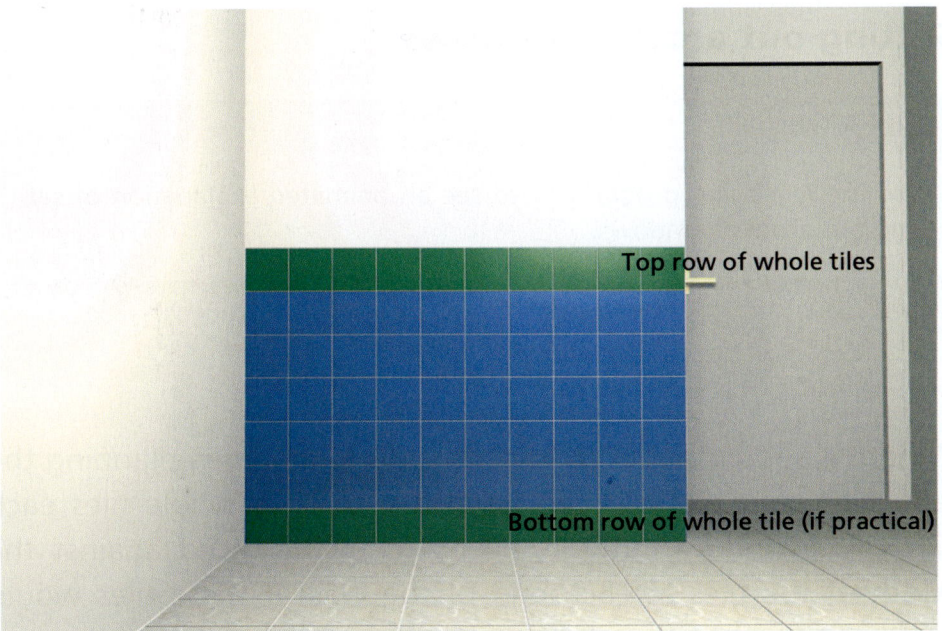

Work out the top and bottom row of tiles

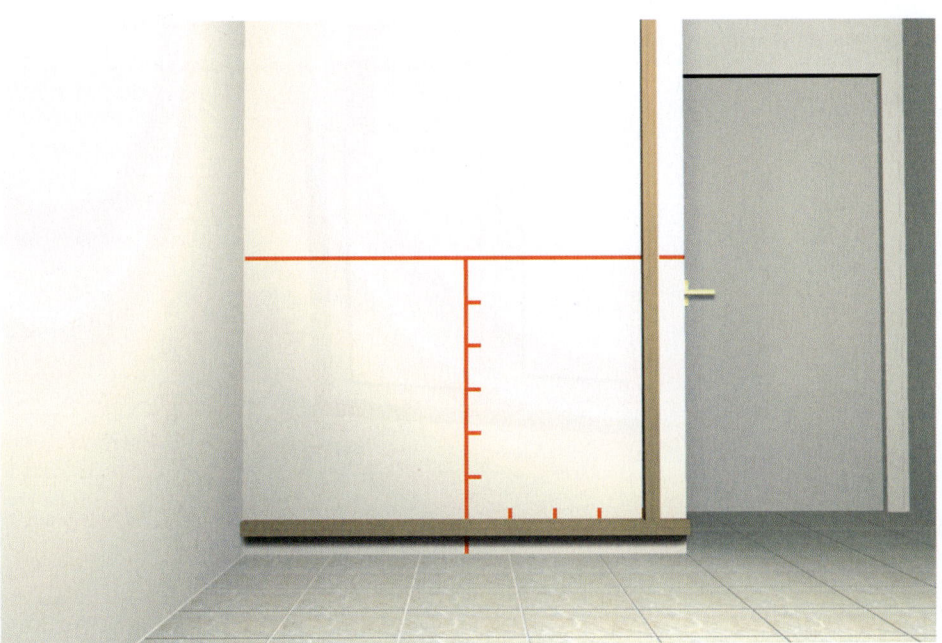

Mark out where your battens are to be placed

Setting out around windows

> **E-LEARNING**
>
> Use the e-learning programme to see an animated explanation of setting out around windows.

Windows should be taken into consideration when planning the layout of your tiling. It can be better to have whole tiles each side of a window but this needs to be balanced against the width of the tiles at each end of the wall. If these tiles would end up being less than half a tile, then cut tiles should be used each side of the window recess. If tiles do need to be cut, there should still be an equal sized tile each side of the window recess.

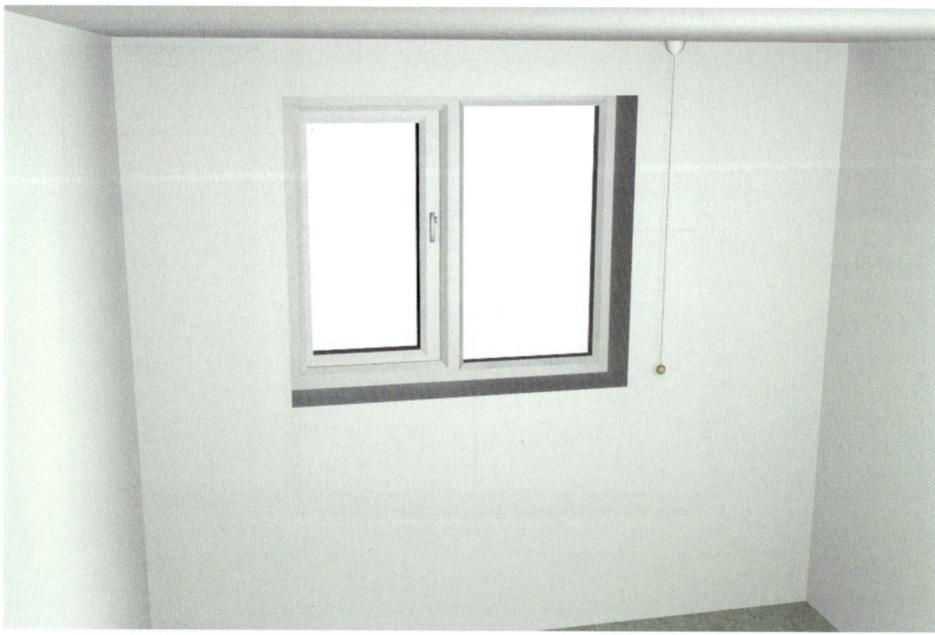

Plan your tiles around the opening

Create a balanced look

Place cut tiles at window recess

When tiling inside the window recess, a whole tile should be placed where the wall meets the recess at 90° and any cut tiles placed inside the recess against the window.

Whole tiles on the outside

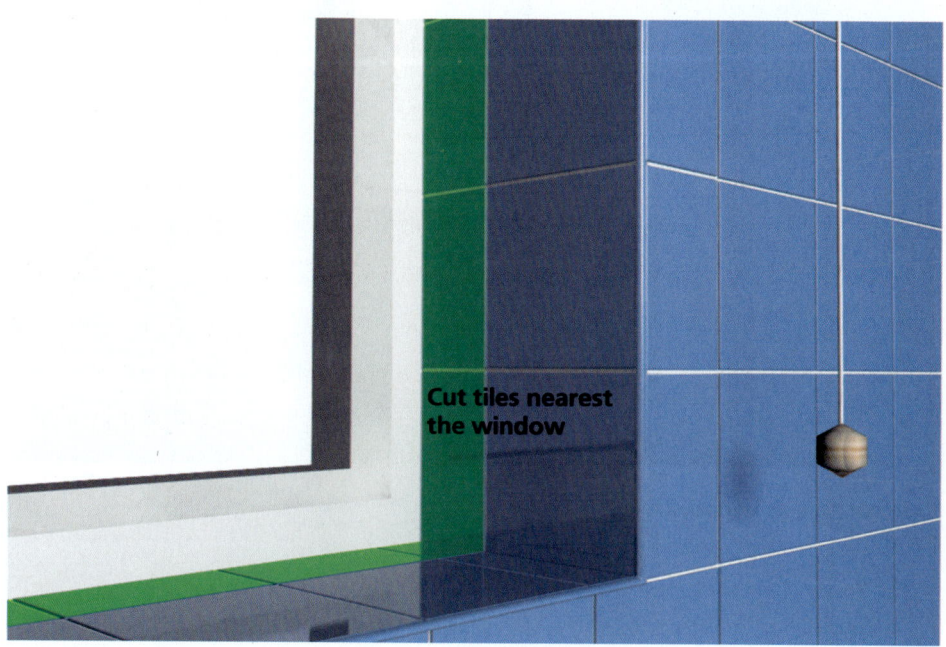

Cut tiles on the inside

CHECK YOUR KNOWLEDGE

1. **When you have marked the centre of a floor to be tiled, why do you need to dry lay tiles along the lines?**

    ☐ a. To ensure the lines are accurate

    ☐ b. To ensure there are no small cut tiles at the edge of the room

    ☐ c. To check you have enough tiles

2. **When setting out a plain wall for tiling, where should the horizontal batten be fixed?**

    ☐ a. Level with the top of the highest row of whole tiles

    ☐ b. Level with the top of the lowest row of whole tiles

    ☐ c. Under the bottom of the lowest row of whole tiles

3. **What are the four steps for marking the vertical guides when marking out a plain wall?**

    1.

    2.

    3.

    4.

4. **Fill in the blanks in the following sentence.**

    For aesthetic reasons, when part tiling a wall, it is better to have a _____ tile at the top and also a _____ tile at the bottom, if this is practical.

5. **True or False: It is essential to have a whole tile each side of a window recess.**

    ☐ a. True

    ☐ b. False

Chapter 4

APPLYING TILES

LEARNING OBJECTIVES

By the end of this chapter you will be able to:

- Explain how adhesive is applied to walls and floors.

- Explain how to lay floor tiles and apply wall tiles.

- Explain how to cut tiles with different tools.

- Explain the process of grouting.

- List a number of trade tips.

CONSTRUCTION: WALL AND FLOOR TILING

NOS REFERENCE

Tile wall and floor surfaces

Produce tiled, mosaic and stone surface finishes

LAYING AND APPLYING TILES

Applying adhesive

E-LEARNING

Use the e-learning programme see an animated explanation of applying adhesive to tiles.

The adhesive required to apply wall and floor tiles will depend on the tiles being used and the background they are being applied to. The manufacturer's recommendations should always be consulted.

Check the type of tile to be used

Check the type of background

For cut tiles, the back of the tile is 'buttered' with adhesive before it is applied to the wall or floor.

Apply adhesive direct to the cut tile

For whole tiles, use your gauging trowel to scoop out the required amount of adhesive and place it on your notched trowel. Then use your notched trowel to spread the adhesive over an area of approximately 1m^2 at a time. The size of notched trowel will depend on the tiles being applied but the notches ensure that an equal amount of adhesive is applied to the whole area.

CONSTRUCTION: WALL AND FLOOR TILING

Cover an area approximately 1m² at any one time

E-LEARNING

Use the e-learning programme to view this information on a slider bar.

Figure	Notch shape (size)	Recommended use
	Square notches (4mm)	Fixing mosaic tiles.
	Square notches (6mm)	Regular sized tiles on internal walls in dry areas.
	Round notches (6mm)	Regular sized tiles on internal walls in dry areas.

APPLYING TILES

Figure	Notch shape (size)	Recommended use
	Square notches (8mm)	Tiles on external walls. Tiles on internal walls in wet areas. Large tiles on internal walls. Small floor tiles.
	Round notches (20mm)	Most floor tiles.

Laying floor tiles

> **E-LEARNING**
>
> Use the e-learning programme to see an animated explanation of laying floor tiles.

Floor adhesive is removed from the container or tub with a gauging trowel, then placed on to the notched trowel. Using the notched trowel spread the adhesive to the floor surface in areas approximately 1m² in size.

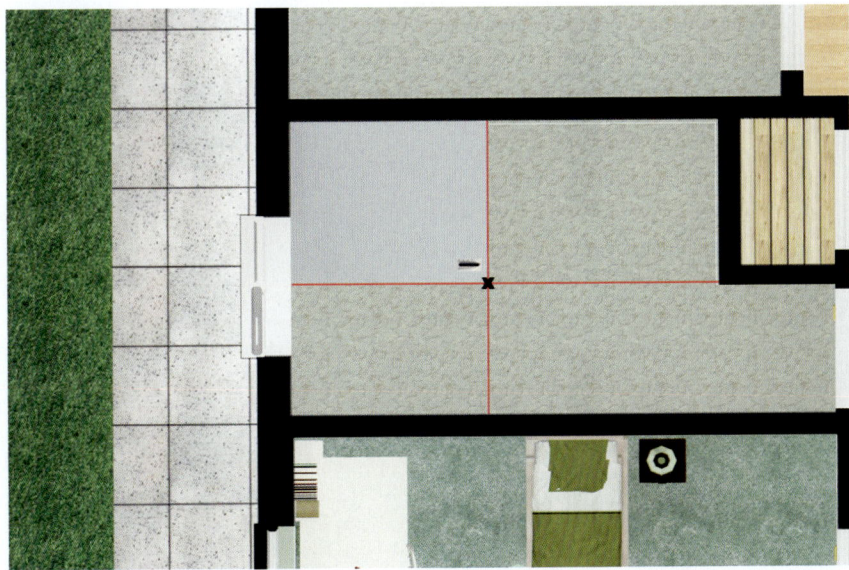

Spread the adhesive on the floor

CONSTRUCTION: WALL AND FLOOR TILING

Floor tiles need to be laid while the adhesive is still effective so plan which sections of the floor you are going to do and in what order, making sure you work back towards the door.

- Using the lines marked on the floor during the setting out process, lay the tiles along the centre line to the wall furthest away from the door.
- Complete the tiles along half of the back wall, forming an L shape.

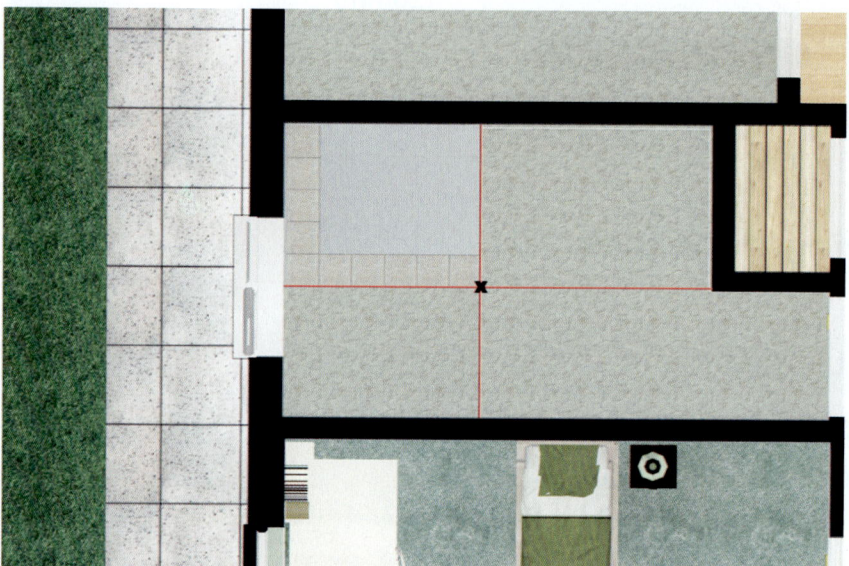

Lay the first line of horizontal and vertical tiles

- Complete a quarter of the room and then move on to the next section leaving yourself a route back to the doorway.

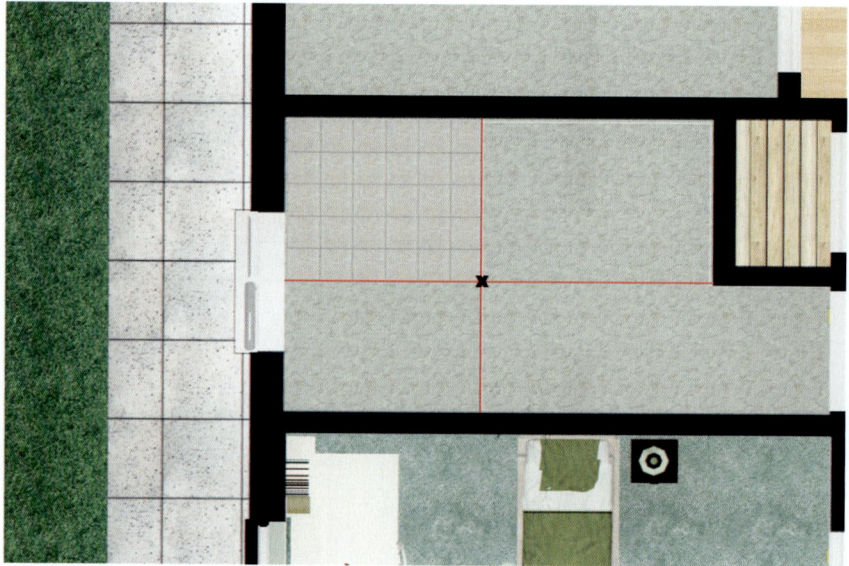

Complete the first quarter

- Check that the tiles are level every few rows and leave all tiles to set fully before grouting.

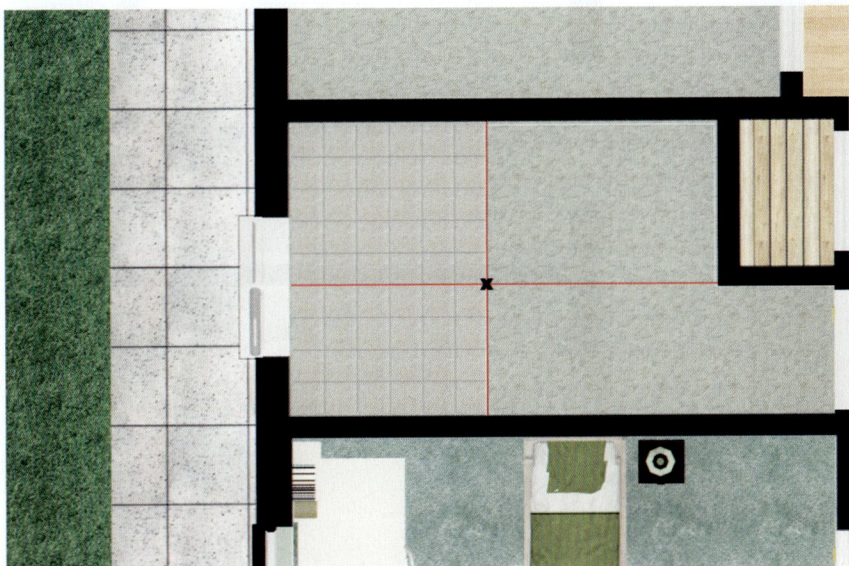

Complete the area furthest from the door

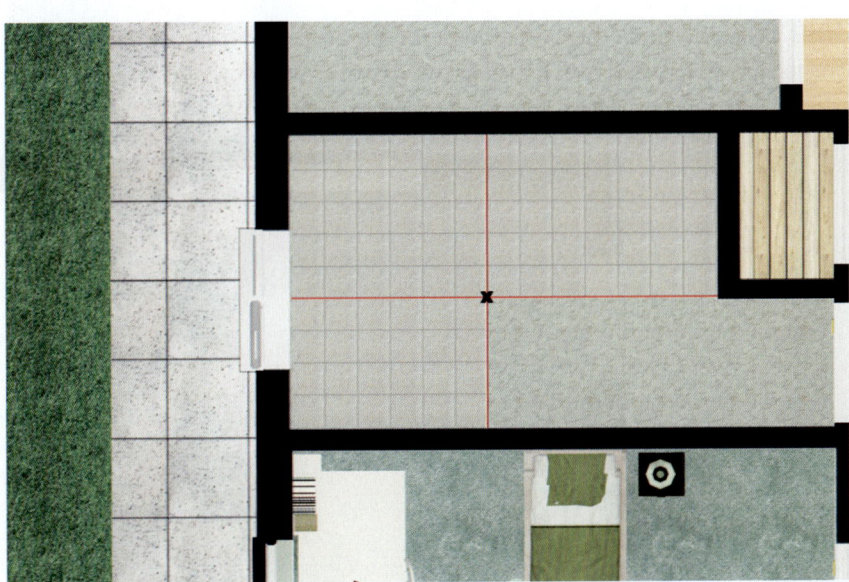

Leave your exit route clear

78 CONSTRUCTION: WALL AND FLOOR TILING

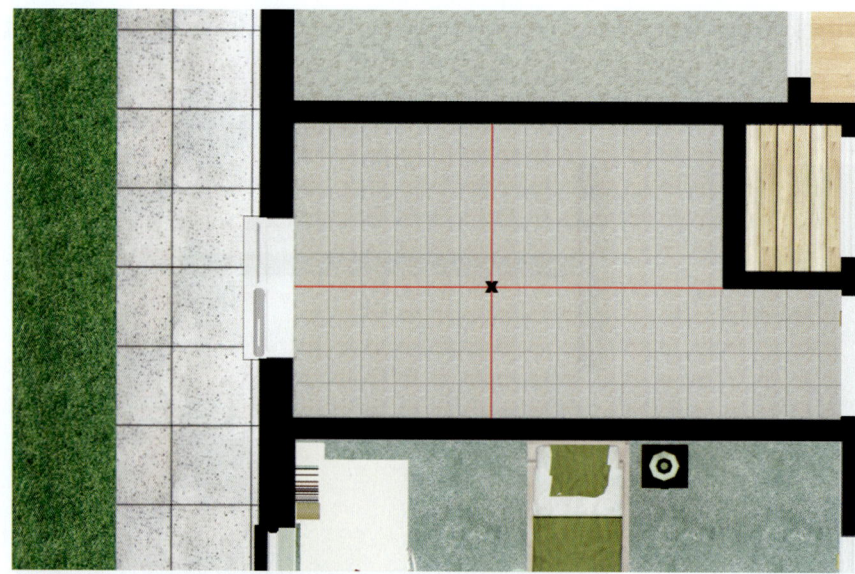

Finish the remaining floor space

ACTIVITY

On this marked out floor, in which order would you tile the sections of the room? Number each quadrant from 1–4 on the image shown.

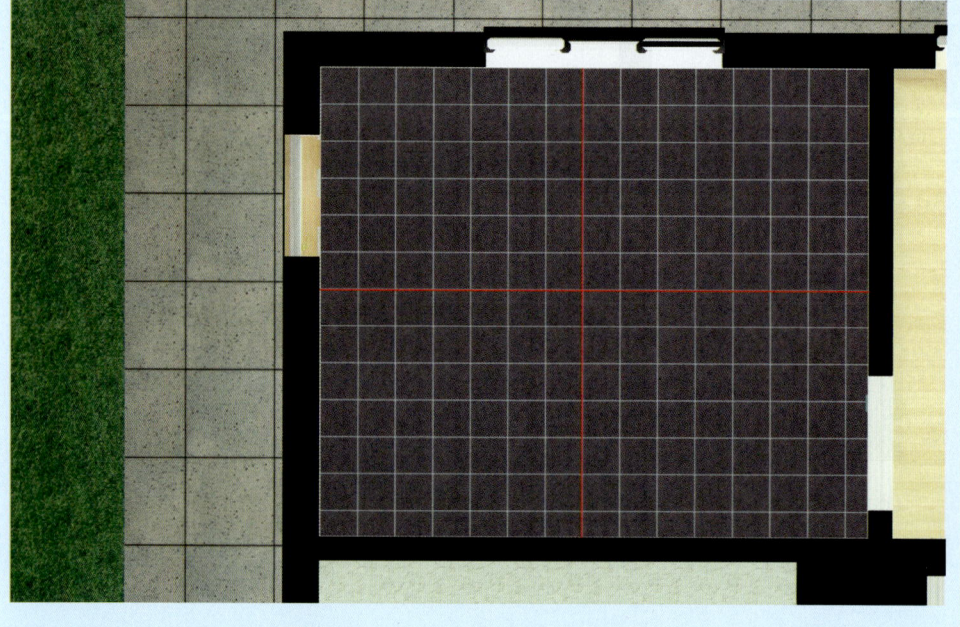

Applying wall tiles

> **E-LEARNING**
>
> Use the e-learning programme to see an animated explanation of applying wall tiles.

Once the adhesive has been applied to the wall, the tiles should be fixed before the adhesive dries out. Applying adhesive in 1m² areas at a time ensures that the tiler has enough time to fix all the tiles before the adhesive becomes too dry and unworkable.

To apply the wall tiles start by following these steps then repeat along the length and height of the wall you are tiling.

- The first whole tile should be placed where the horizontal and vertical battens meet, twisting the tile slightly as it is pressed into the adhesive to increase the contact between the tile and the background.

Place the first tile at the corner of the battens

CONSTRUCTION: WALL AND FLOOR TILING

- The second tile is fixed next to the first using a spacer to allow a gap for grouting.

Use the tile spacers to position further tiles

- Once the first row of whole tiles is complete continue working upwards one row at a time until all the whole tiles have been applied.

Work upwards row by row

- The vertical and horizontal level of the tiles should be checked every few rows and while the adhesive is still flexible enough to allow the tiles to be moved if necessary.

Check tiles are level and straight

- Once complete, the whole tiles should be left to dry completely before the battens are removed and the cut tiles are applied.

Leave tiles to dry

CONSTRUCTION: WALL AND FLOOR TILING

Remove battens and add remaining tiles

CUTTING TILES

> **E-LEARNING**
>
> Use the e-learning programme to see an animated explanation of how to use each tool.

Tile scorer

For a straight cut on a small tile, measure the size of the tile needed, remembering to allow space for grouting, and mark this line on the face of the tile using a water soluble felt pen or **chinagraph pencil**. The tile can now be cut by scoring along the line with a tile scorer and then snapping the tile across a wooden batten.

Chinagraph pencil A coloured wax pencil that can be used to mark hard surfaces. The marks made by the pencil are moisture resistant but can be removed with a cloth or towel.

APPLYING TILES 83

Mark where the cut needs to be made

Run the tile scorer along the mark

CONSTRUCTION: WALL AND FLOOR TILING

Snap the tile over a batten

Tile cutter

For larger tiles a tile cutter can be used instead of a tile scorer. Place the tile into the cutter, taking care to line it up accurately. Run the scoring wheel across the tile, then use the jaws of the cutter to press down and snap the tile leaving a straight and clean cut.

Place the tile in the cutter

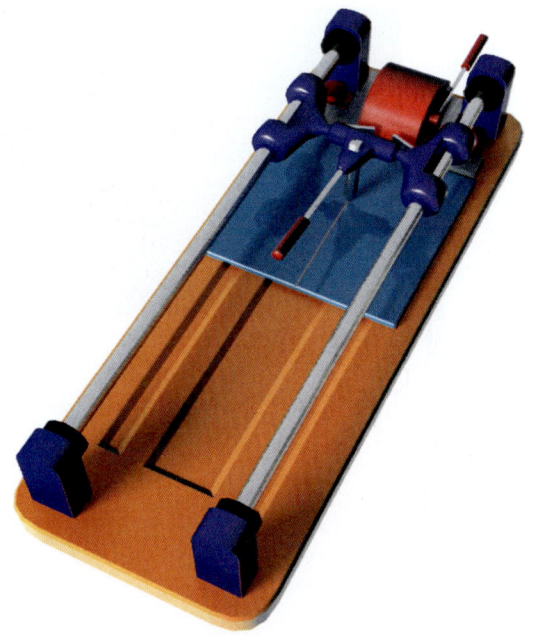

Mark the tile with the scoring wheel

Snap the tile in the jaws of the cutter

Nibblers

If the cut is straight but only a small amount needs to be removed from a small tile, it is easier to use nibblers. Score a line where the tile needs to be cut and use the nibblers to remove small amounts of tile until the scored line is reached. L-shaped tiles around openings or socket boxes can also be cut in this way.

86 CONSTRUCTION: WALL AND FLOOR TILING

Mark where the cut needs to be made

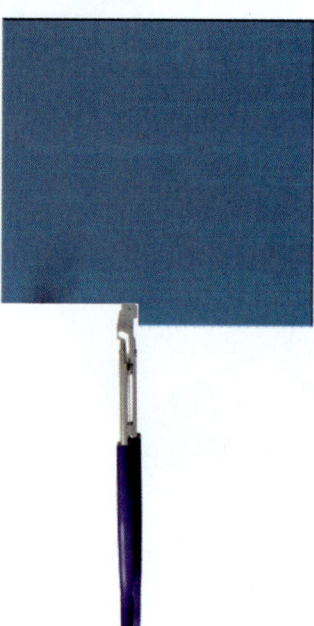

Snip parts of the tile away

APPLYING TILES 87

Use for trimming tiles

Rod saw

For curves or more complicated cuts in small tiles, a rod saw can be used. Similar to a hacksaw it allows flexibility and can cut in any direction. Create a cardboard or paper template of the cut and then transfer this pattern on to the surface of the tile. Make sure the tile is securely fastened to a work bench before cutting.

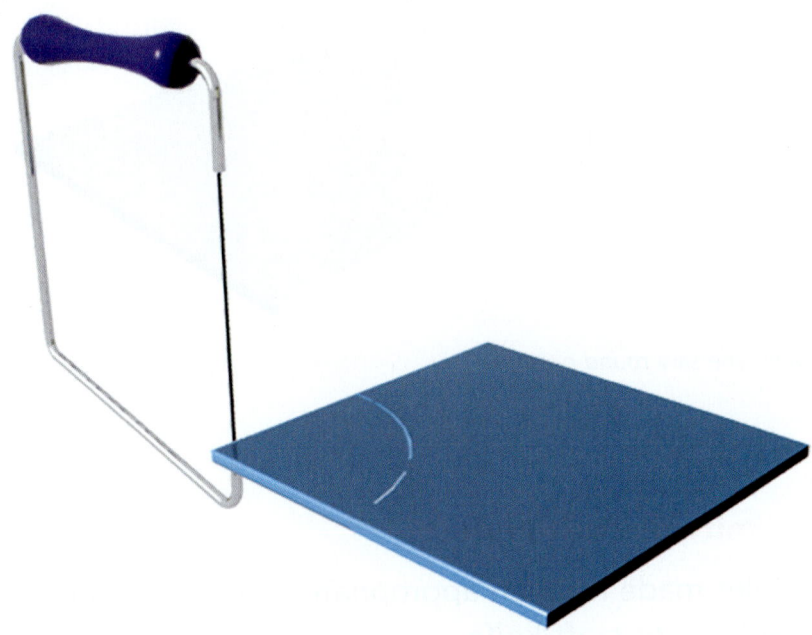

Mark the tile with a template

CONSTRUCTION: WALL AND FLOOR TILING

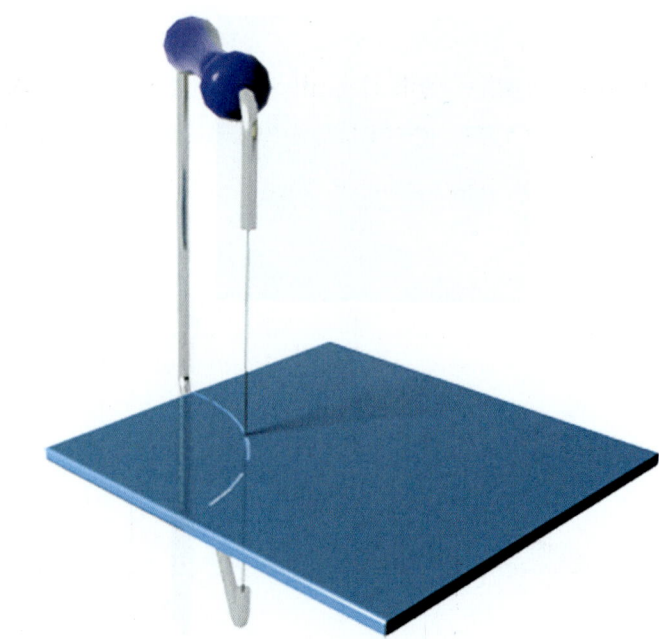

Secure tile to workbench before cutting

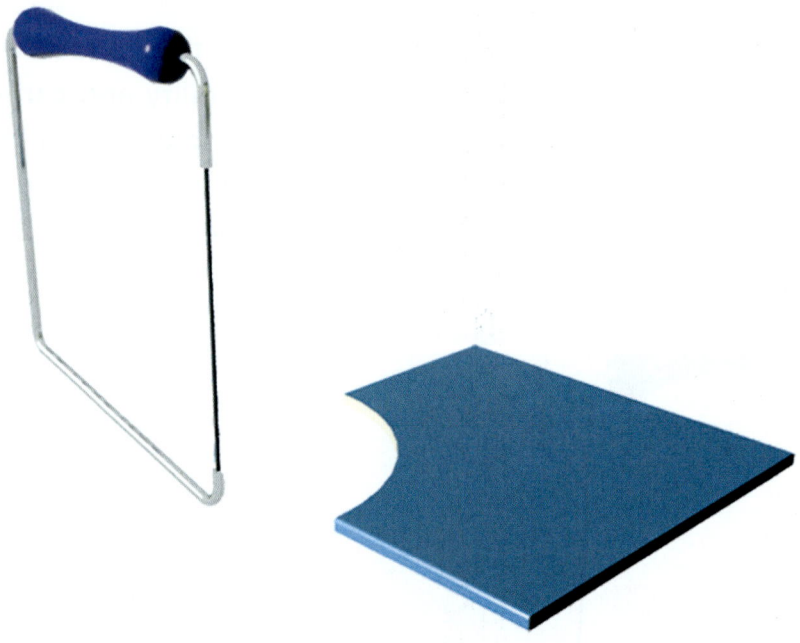

Move the saw round carefully

Stanley knife or craft knife

Thinner tiles made from an appropriate material can be cut with a Stanley knife or craft knife.

APPLYING TILES

Wet saw

Stronger and thicker tiles will usually need to be cut with a wet saw. This uses a motorized circular blade which cuts through the tile whilst being splashed with water.

Line up tile

Be extremely careful and take all precautions when cutting

CONSTRUCTION: WALL AND FLOOR TILING

Hole saw

A **hole saw** is a **drill bit** that can be of varying sizes which is attached to the drill and used to cut circular holes in tiles. You should apply gentle pressure and use the pilot bit as a guide when cutting through.

Hole saw A drill bit that can be of varying sizes that is attached to the drill and used to cut circular holes in tiles. You should apply gentle pressure and use the pilot bit as a guide when cutting through.

Drill bit A cutting tool which fits securely into the drill to create a cylindrical hole.

Use the correct size drill bit

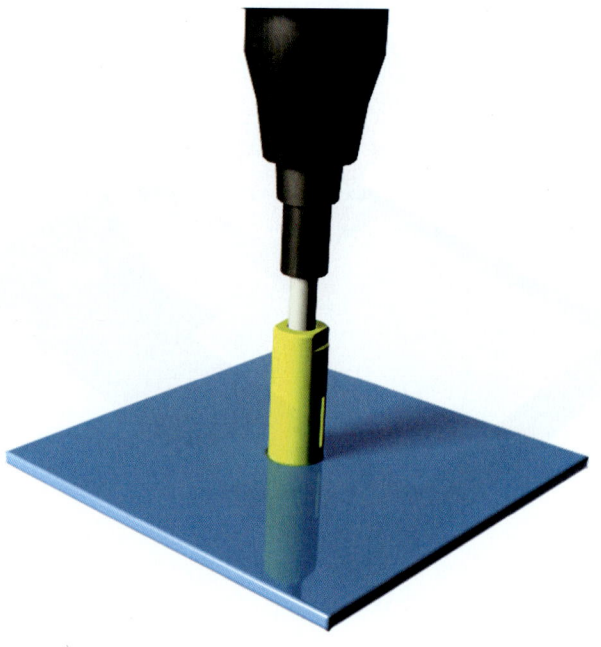

Cut through tile with caution

Turn off drill and remove cut tile

HEALTH & SAFETY

You should always wear the required **PPE** and use caution when using any cutting tools.

PPE The standard and widely used abbreviation for Personal Protective Equipment.

ACTIVITY

Which tool(s) would you use to cut the floor tiles around a lavatory or washbasin pedestal and how do you think you would carry out this task? Write your answers below.

Tiling around windows

> **E-LEARNING**
>
> Use the e-learning programme to see an animated explanation of tiling around windows.

If during the setting out process, you find you need a cut tile above a window recess it is easier to fix a batten at the bottom of the lowest row of whole tiles above the window and tile upwards from this point. Once the whole tiles are fixed and dry, the batten can be removed and the cut tiles applied. This also applies to other fixtures like baths, basins and worktops.

When tiling around windows specifically, the cut tiles applied above the recess will have no support underneath while they are drying so can be held in place with masking tape until they are completely dry. A rapid setting adhesive can be used as an alternative.

Attach a horizontal batten

APPLYING TILES 93

Fix whole tiles

Remove horizontal batten

CONSTRUCTION: WALL AND FLOOR TILING

Fix cut tiles

Cutting floor tiles

E-LEARNING

Use the e-learning programme to see an animated explanation of cutting floor tiles.

To mark the cuts on floor tiles at the border of a room:

- Dry lay a whole tile in its final position and then lay another whole tile on top of it with the edge lined up against the wall.
- If you are cutting **vinyl** tiles mark the lower tile against the edge of the upper tile; if you are marking other tiles remember to add on the width of the tile spacer.
- The lower tile will now be marked to fit exactly at the edge of the room.

The same method can be used to mark L-shaped cuts in tiles to fit corners, but a cardboard or paper template is used to create a pattern for more complicated cuts which is transferred to the tile before cutting.

Vinyl A soft, flexible and cushioned flooring available in sheets or tiles.

APPLYING TILES 95

Place tile over another

Mark where it needs to be cut

CONSTRUCTION: WALL AND FLOOR TILING

Method also used for 'L' or corner shapes

Use a template for curves

GROUTING

Preparing and applying grout

> **E-LEARNING**
>
> Use the e-learning programme to see an animated explanation of applying grout.

Before grouting tiles, the adhesive must be completely dry. There are many types of grout available so it is important that the correct one is selected for the location where it is to be used, and the manufacturer's recommendations should be followed.

Grout should be mixed in small quantities, enough to cover approximately 1m² areas at a time. It should be mixed to a smooth paste in a clean bucket with clean cold water.

Grout is applied to the tiles using a **grout float** in all directions to force the grout completely into the joints. Like adhesive, it is best to work in areas of 1m² to ensure the grout doesn't dry before it is in place.

> **Grout float** A float with a rubber base used for grouting floor and wall tiles. The grout is placed on the grout float and not the surface when applying.

Apply grout in all directions

Finishing grouting

> **E-LEARNING**
>
> Use the e-learning programme to see an animated explanation of finishing grout.

Excess grout should be removed from the tiles before it is dry using a clean damp grout sponge washed in a bucket of clean cold water. The joints can then be finished using a specialist grout finisher or the rounded end of a dowel rod.

When you have completed the grouting there will be a thin layer of grout left on the surface of the tiles. This can be removed by polishing the tiles with a dry cloth once the grout is dry.

Remove excess grout

APPLYING TILES 99

Smooth and finish off the grout between tiles

Remove thin layer of grout and polish tiles

Sealing joints

> **E-LEARNING**
>
> Use the e-learning programme to see an animated explanation of sealing joints.

When you have finished grouting you will need to seal joints between surfaces, e.g. the joint between the tiles and the bath. You can use a mastic silicone sealant which is available in different colours and it is a good idea to fill the bath three-quarters full first to simulate the weight of normal usage:

- Make sure that the area is completely clean and free of any dust and that any old, existing mastic has been fully removed.
- Cut the nozzle of the tube, usually at an angle, then fit the tube to a **sealant gun**.
- Tilt the gun and place the nozzle with the angled edge against the joint.
- Start from one corner and apply a gentle even pressure moving continuously at a steady speed to the other end.
- Try to avoid a wide joint.
- Smooth down the mastic, cleaning up any areas and leave to set.

Sealant gun A device used for the application of sealant.

Seal any gaps between tiles and other surfaces

TRADE TIPS

E-LEARNING

Use the e-learning programme to view this information in a flip book.

ACTIVITY

There are a number of trade tips that can make tiling easier. What tips can you suggest for the following headings? Write your answers below.

Planning

Floor tiling

Wall tiling

Grouting and sealing

APPLYING TILES 101

CHECK YOUR KNOWLEDGE

1. For the best results, to what size area should adhesive be applied?

   ☐ a. 1m²

   ☐ b. 2m²

   ☐ c. 3m²

2. True or False: When tiling above a window, the cut tiles should be applied first.

   ☐ a. True

   ☐ b. False

3. Before sealing around a bath, how much water should you run in the bath?

   ☐ a. Quarter full

   ☐ b. Half full

   ☐ c. Three-quarters full

   ☐ d. Up to the brim

4. List four different tools that can be used to cut tiles.

   1.

   2.

   3.

   4.

5. When should adhesive be applied to the back of the tile instead of to the background?

   ☐ a. Always

   ☐ b. When applying a cut tile

   ☐ c. Never

Chapter 5

END TEST

END TEST OBJECTIVES

The end test will check your knowledge on the information held within this workbook.

The Test

E-LEARNING
Use the e-learning programme to complete this test online.

1. **Which of the following tasks is a tiler expected to carry out?**
   - ☐ a. Measure and set out areas for tiling
   - ☐ b. Fix and install fittings and furniture
   - ☐ c. Fix, cut and grout tiles
   - ☐ d. Fit plasterboard walls ready for tiling

2. **What combined weight of tiles, adhesive and grout can each of these backgrounds approximately support?**

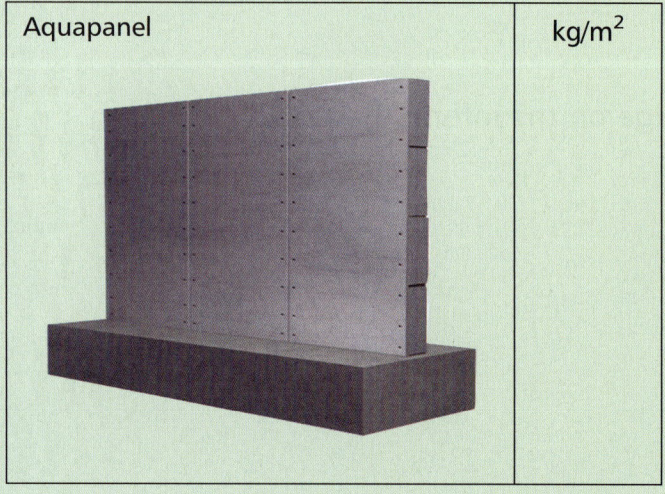

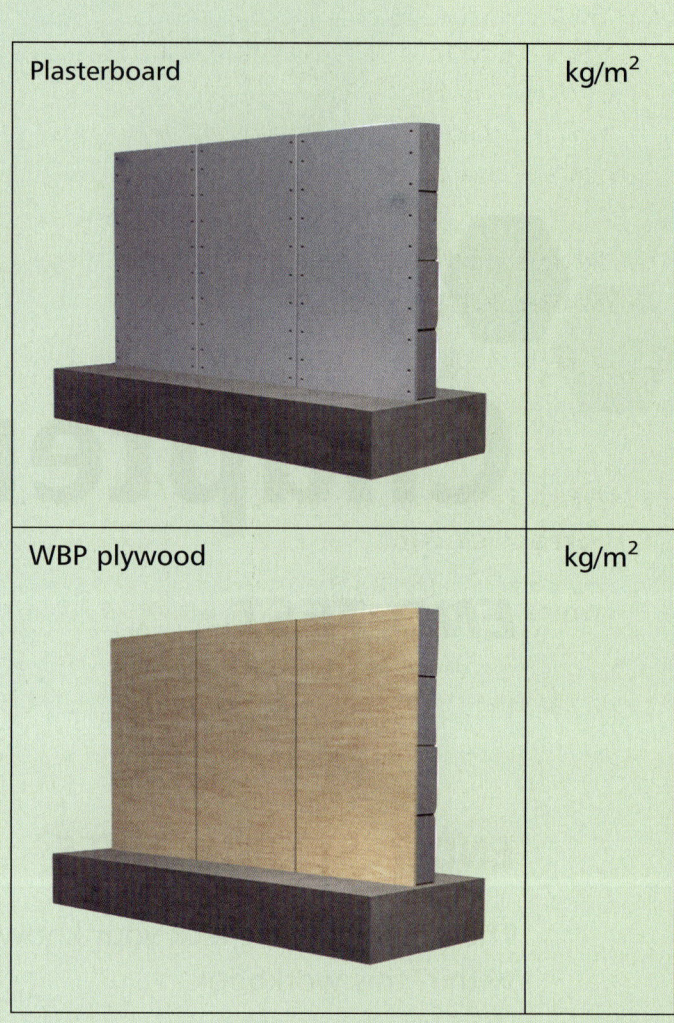

3. **How should tiles be stored?**
   - ☐ a. Flat and raised off the ground
   - ☐ b. Flat and on the ground
   - ☐ c. On their side raised off the ground
   - ☐ d. On their side on the ground

4. **How many boxes of 100 × 150mm tiles do you need to cover an area of 6.75m² with 10 per cent wastage? Note: 1 box of 67, 100 × 150mm tiles covers an area of 0.76m².**

5. **Which of these tools would be used in the setting out process?**

- [ ] a. Gauge rod
- [ ] b. Grout float
- [ ] c. Spirit level
- [ ] d. Tile adhesive
- [ ] e. Gauging trowel

6. **Glazed ceramic tiles are suitable for high traffic areas.**

- [ ] a. True
- [ ] b. False

7. **What is the process for marking out a plain wall? Number the actions in the correct order.**

Steps	Actions
	Mark the position of the top of the lowest row of tiles
	Fix a batten at this point
	Measure the height of the wall and mark the horizontal centre across the wall
	Adjust centre line if bottom tile is less than ½ tile
	Use a tile gauge to mark the position of tiles down to floor level
	Check this line with a level

8. **When part-tiling a wall, which of these are the preferred options?**

- [ ] a. Whole tile at the bottom, cut tile at the top
- [ ] b. Whole tile at the top and at the bottom
- [ ] c. Whole tile at the top, cut tile at the bottom

9. **When tiling in a window recess, where should the whole tile be placed?**

- [ ] a. Nearest the window
- [ ] b. Where the window recess meets the wall

10. **Where should the first line be marked when marking out a floor for tiling?**

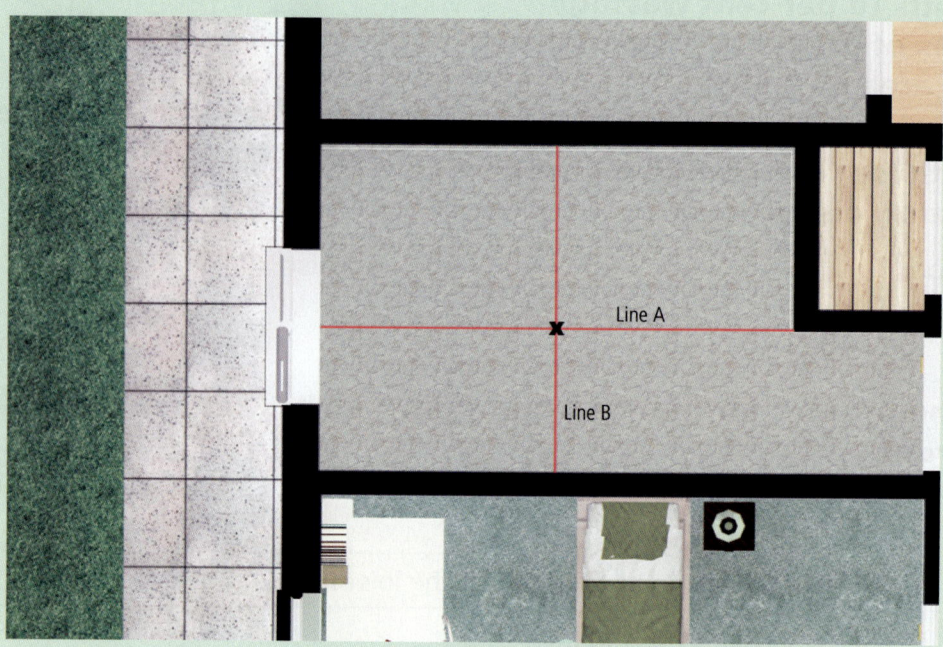

- a. Line A
- b. Line B

11. **When tiling a shower or wet room floor, what should the minimum fall be from the edge of the shower to the drain?**

12. **In which sequence should you apply tiles to a wall surface prepared with adhesive in a 1m² area?**
    - a. Vertically one column at a time
    - b. Horizontally one row at a time
    - c. In blocks

13. **Where should cut marks be made on a tile?**
    - a. On the face of the tile
    - b. On the reverse of the tile

14. **Grout can be applied immediately after laying floor tiles.**
    - a. True
    - b. False

15. When laying a floor, which of the following tasks should you carry out?

☐ a. Leave a route back to the door
☐ b. Start from the door entrance
☐ c. Lay the tiles in the middle of the room and work outwards
☐ d. Lay tiles in areas of a manageable size
☐ e. Allow to dry completely before grouting

Answers to Check Your Knowledge and End Test

CHAPTER 1

1. **B:** A plumb, true and level background will not have any gaps of more than 3mm between points of contact over a distance of 2m.

2. **False:** Tiling is a second fix trade.

3. **False:** A plasterboard background can support up to 32kg/m^2.

4. Letter, email.

5. The background should be specified as 'to be tiled' in the design specification to ensure a plumb, true and level surface.

CHAPTER 2

1. Gloves, goggles, knee pads and a dust mask are recommended when using tile adhesives and grouts.

2. To cover an area of 4m^2, you need 4 boxes of 200 × 250mm tiles.

1 box covers	1.25m^2
Tile area	4m^2
Boxes required	4m^2/1.25m^2 = 3.2
10 per cent wastage	3.2 × 10/100 = 0.32
Total boxes required	= 4 (rounded up)

3. **False.** Tiles that have been stored outside should be allowed to acclimatize to room temperature before they are laid to prevent them cracking.

4. Dry cloth, grout finisher, grout float, grout remover, grout sponge, sealant.

5. Waste minimization strategies include reduce, reuse and recycle.

CHAPTER 3

1. **B:** You dry lay tiles along the lines to ensure there are no small cut tiles at the edge of the room.

2. **C:** You should fix the horizontal batten under the bottom of the lowest row of whole tiles when setting out a plain wall for tiling.

3. (1) Mark the centre of the wall. (2) Mark out the vertical rows of tiles using your tile gauge until you reach the point at which the last whole tile falls. (3) Use a level to ensure this line is plumb. (4) Attach a vertical batten at this point.

4. For aesthetic reasons, when part tiling a wall, it is better to have a whole tile at the top and also a whole tile at the bottom if this is practical.

5. False: It can be better to have whole tiles each side of a window but this needs to be balanced against the width of the tiles at each end of the wall. If these tiles would end up being less than half a tile, then cut tiles should be used each side of the window recess.

CHAPTER 4

1. A: When applying adhesive you should cover an area of approximately 1m² at a time. This gives the tiler enough time to lay the tiles before the adhesive becomes unworkable.

2. False: You should apply the whole tiles around the window first as this will indicate the size of the cut tiles needed.

3. C: Before sealing a bath, fill it three-quarters full of water first, this will allow for movement when the bath is being used.

4. Tile scorer, nibblers, rod saw, Stanley (craft) knife, wet saw.

5. B: For cut tiles, the back of the tile is 'buttered' with adhesive before it is applied to the wall or floor.

CHAPTER 5

Check your answers against the following. If any of the questions you answered are incorrect you are advised to go back to that section in the workbook or the e-learning programme to re-study.

Question 1

A and C: A tiler is expected to measure and set out areas for tiling as well as fix, cut and grout tiles.

Question 2

Aquapanel	50kg/m²
Plasterboard	32kg/m²
WBP plywood	30kg/m²

Question 3

A and C: Tiles can be stored flat or on their sides but must always be raised off the ground.

Question 4

10.

To cover an area of 6.75m² you need 10 boxes of 100 × 100mm tiles.

1 box covers 0.76m².

Tile area = 6.75m², boxes required = 6.75m²/0.760m² = 8.88.

10 per cent wastage = 8.88 × 10/100 = 0.89.

Total boxes required = 9.77, rounded up to 10.

Question 5

A and C: A gauge rod and spirit level would be used as part of the setting out process.

Question 6

False: Glazed ceramic tiles are not suitable for high traffic areas as they can be easily damaged by the grit brought in on footwear.

Question 7

1 = Measure the height of the wall and mark the horizontal centre across the wall.

2 = Use a tile gauge to mark the position of tiles down to floor level.

3 = Adjust centre line if bottom tile is less than ½ tile.

4 = Mark the position of the top of the lowest row of tiles.

5 = Check this line with a level.

6 = Fix a batten at this point.

Question 8

B and C: There should always be a whole tile at the top and if possible a whole tile at the bottom.

Question 9

B: When tiling in a window recess, the whole tile should be placed where the window recess meets the wall.

Question 10

Line A: The first line to be marked should join the centre points of the two shortest walls in the room.

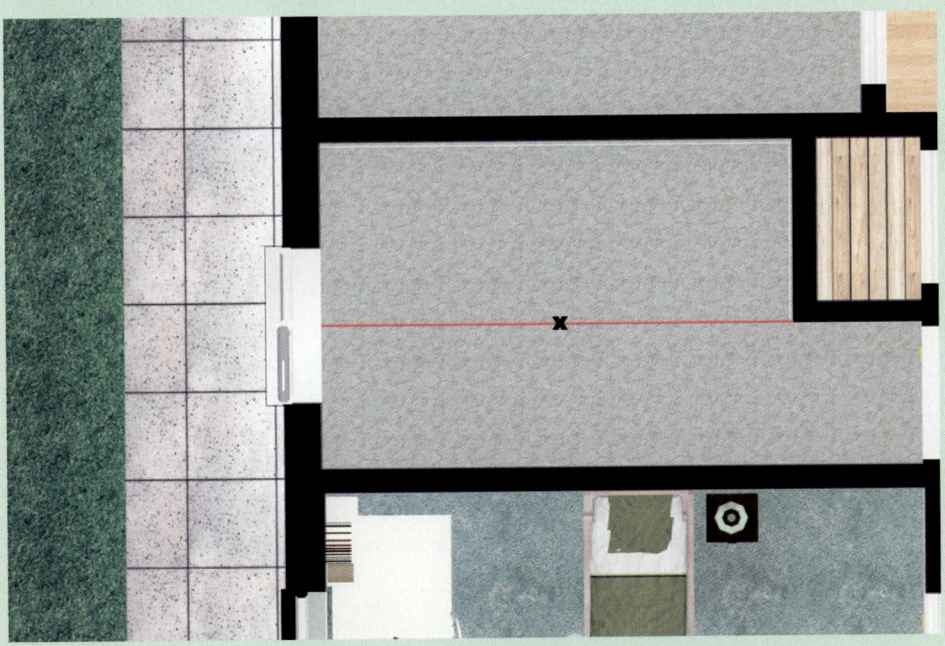

Question 11

75mm: To ensure the water drains efficiently, the fall from the edge of the shower to the drain should be a minimum of 75mm.

Question 12

B: Tiles should be applied horizontally one row at a time.

Question 13

A: Cut marks should be made on the face of the tile.

Question 14

False: Tile adhesive should be allowed to dry for at least 24 hours before grouting.

Question 15

A, D and E: When laying a floor, you should: leave a route back to the door, lay tiles in areas of manageable size and allow the tiles to dry completely before grouting.

Glossary

Adhesive General term for a range of bonding agents.

Backgrounds General term used for the surface to which materials are adhered.

Batten (tiling) Timber strip fixed to the wall to support the first course of whole tiles.

Cement A grey or white powdery material made from chalk or limestone and clay. Cement is the most common binder in bricklaying mortar and works by hardening as a result of a chemical reaction when mixed with water. The most common type of cement is Ordinary Portland Cement (OPC).

Chalk line A length of string, coated in chalk dust, which is used to produce accurate straight lines. The line is held at both ends and snapped against a surface thus transferring chalk dust to it.

Chinagraph pencil A coloured wax pencil that can be used to mark hard surfaces. The marks made by the pencil are moisture resistant but can be removed with a cloth or towel.

Drill bit A cutting tool which fits securely into the drill to create a cylindrical hole.

Float A range of tools which can be made from a variety of materials with a grip that holds a thin flat base approximately 100mm × 250mm. There are a number of different floats for different purposes including plasterer's float, devil float and grout float.

Floor screed The final layer of concrete laid on top of the oversite concrete to level off. The floor screed is usually laid later on in the project.

Gauge stick A timber batten marked with tile size measurements to help establish the most acceptable setting out on each wall.

Gauging trowel A popular trowel used for the mixing, bedding and placing of materials.

Glazed A ceramic coating in a glassy state or the material from which this coating is made.

Grout A cement-based filler, available in a range of colours and formulated with varying sized fine aggregates to fill the joints between tiles. Some grouts can be waterproof.

Grout finisher A tool used for smoothing out grout joints and sealants.

Grout float A float with a rubber base used for grouting floor and wall tiles. The grout is placed on the grout float and not on the surface when applying.

Grout remover A tool used for removing old grouts before re-grouting during renovation projects.

Grout sponge A sponge with rounded edges for removing excess grout on tiles during grouting.

Hole saw A drill bit that can be of varying sizes that is attached to the drill and used to cut circular holes in tiles. You should apply gentle pressure and use the pilot bit as a guide when cutting through.

Keys The preparation to backgrounds either chemically, mechanically, hacking or scratching before plaster or render is applied. Creating keys ensure that the plaster or render sticks and the method of keying will depend on the type of background.

GLOSSARY

Laser level A mechanical device mounted on a stand which extends to the height of the room. The laser level projects the horizontal and vertical levels on to the surface using laser beams.

Level The horizontal level of a surface or structure.

Mastic adhesive An alternate adhesive suitable for tiling walls as it has a quicker initial 'grab'. The limitation of mastic adhesive is that it is only suitable for thin bed application which makes it unsuitable for tiling floors.

Nibbler A hand tool used to cut tiles by making a series of small cuts to achieve a particular shape or size. After cutting, a tile file should be used to smooth the edges.

Notched trowel A trowel used for the even application of adhesives to walls and floors. Notches come in different size and shapes and the correct notched trowel to use will depend on the tile being fixed.

Personal Protective Equipment (PPE) Depending on the type of work, there are different types of equipment specifically designed to protect your health and safety. Examples include gloves, safety boots, goggles and dust mask.

Plaster A colourless, white or pinkish mineral formed from heating gypsum at high temperatures. Plaster is used to protect and enhance the appearance of a surface as it provides a joint-less finish.

Plasterboard A type of board made of gypsum sandwiched between sheets of paper. It has a number of properties and can be made to different thicknesses and sizes for different areas and uses.

Plumb The vertical level of a surface or structure.

Polyvinyl Acetate A type of bonding agent commonly known as PVA.

PPE The standard and widely used abbreviation for Personal Protective Equipment (see definition above).

PVA The standard and widely used abbreviation for Polyvinyl Acetate (see definition above).

Reference lines Two lines intersecting at 90° that are marked on a wall or floor during setting out for tiling, in order to establish a starting point for layout lines to assist the placing of tiles.

Render A sand and cement backing coat for tiling, usually applied in at least two coats.

Sand Fine aggregate that is one of the raw ingredients for mixing mortar.

Sealant A filler that is used for covering joints in tiles where grouting is not suitable. For example, corners, sinks, baths and other wet areas.

Sealant gun A device used for the application of sealant.

Set square A tool used for marking or checking right angle lines.

Setting out The process of planning how the tiles are going to be laid out on a surface. It includes measuring your surface areas, checking the laying of tiles, planning the tile order and making sure everything is plumb and level.

Spirit level A tool used to check true vertical and horizontal lines indicated by a bubble in spirit-filled vials.

Sustainable materials Materials that have been sourced by causing little or no damage to the environment.

Tile file A tool used to smooth off edges after a tile has been cut.

Tile scorer A tool with a needle used to score a mark on the face of a tile. The tile can then be snapped across a wooden batten.

Tile spacers Small plastic shapes that fit between the tiles as they are being laid to ensure an even professional finish. They are available in a number of different sizes and the size required will depend on the size of tile being used.

GLOSSARY

Tile trim Edgings that protect the edges of tiles that meet at 90° and also create a professional finish. They are used on internal and external corners.

Underfloor heating A type of heating provided by water pipes or electric elements in the screed or electric mats on the floor screed under a floor. Underfloor heating can be used under tiled floors.

Vinyl flooring A soft, flexible and cushioned flooring available in sheets or tiles.

Water level A tool used for transferring levels from one wall or room to another. This tool consists of two plastic water containers, tubing filled with water and an air release valve on a gauge rod. The same level on the walls in two different rooms can be achieved by matching the water level of each of the water containers to the same level.

Wet saw A tool used for cutting thicker tiles. This saw has a motorized circular blade which cuts through the tile whilst being splashed with water.

Index

adhesive 24–5, 113
   applying 72–5
      removal from container or tub 75
   tools for 39

backgrounds 24, 113
batten (tiling) 32, 113

calculating material quantities 43–4
carbon footprint 46
cement 24, 113
chalk line 34, 113
chinagraph pencil 82, 113
cutting tiles
   around windows 92–4
   floor tiles 94–6
   tools 82–91

devil float 40
disposal of materials 48–9
drill bit 90, 113
dry cloth 41
dust mask 26

float 40, 113
floor screed 113
floor tiles
   checking the lines 57–8
   cutting 94–6
   laying 75–8
   marking out a floor 54–7
   setting out 54–9
   shower and wet room 59

gauge stick 33, 113
gauging trowel 39, 113
glazed 20, 113
glazed ceramic tiles 20
goggles 26
grout 25, 113
grout finisher 41, 113
grout float 40, 97, 113
grout remover 42, 113

grout sponge 40–1, 113
grouting
   finishing 98–9
   preparing and applying 97
   tools 40–2

health & safety
   clothing 26, 91
   handling techniques 48
hole saw 90, 113

joint sealing 100

keys 113
kneepads 26

landfill 48
laser level 31, 114
laying floor tiles 75–8
level 30, 114

mallet 38
marking out
   floors 54–7
   horizontal guides 61–2
   part-tiled walls 64–5
   plain walls 60–4
   vertical guides 63–4
mastic adhesive 25, 114
mosaic tiles 21

nibbler 36, 85–7, 114
notched trowel 39, 114

ordering materials 43–4

part-tiled walls 64–5
personal protective equipment (PPE) 91, 114
plain walls 60–4
plaster 114
plasterboard 114
plasterer's float 40

plumb 30, 114
polyvinyl acetate (PVA) 114
porcelain tiles 21
PPE see personal protective equipment
PVA see polyvinyl acetate

quarry tiles 21

reduce, reuse, recycle materials 49
reference lines 114
render 114
rod saw 37, 87–8
rotary level 31
ruler (or tape) measure 32–3

sand 114
sealant 42, 114
sealant gun 100, 114
sealing joints 100
set square 33–4, 114
setting out 30, 114
   around windows 66–8
   floor tiles 54–9
   wall tiles 59–68
shower room tiles 59
skin irritation 26
slate tiles 22
sourcing materials 46
spacers 27–8
spirit level 30–1, 114
Stanley knife 88
storage of materials 47–8
sustainability 46, 48–9
sustainable materials 20, 114

tile cutter 36, 84–5
tile file 36, 114
tile scorer 36–7, 82–3, 114
tile spacers 27–8, 114
tile trim 28–30, 115
tiles
   applying adhesive 72–4

laying 75–9
sizes 23
storing 47–8
tools for cutting and fixing 35–8
types 20–2
tools
    for adhesives 39
    for cutting and fixing 35–8
    for grouting 40–2
    for setting out 30–4
trade tips 101
trims 28–30

underfloor heating 115
unglazed ceramic tiles 21

ventilation 26
vinyl flooring 94, 115

wall tiles
    applying 79–82
    around windows 66–8
    considerations 59–60
    horizontal guides 61–2
    marking out part-tiled walls 64–5
    marking out plain walls 60–4
    setting out 59–68
    vertical guides 63–4
waste minimization strategies 49
water level 31–2, 115
wet room tiles 59
wet saw 37, 89, 115
windows
    setting out around 66–8
    tiling around 92–4